Janet
Hope you
enjoy the book

"A REFRESHINGLY DIFFERENT APPROACH TO WINNING ON LINKEDIN"

ELEVATE
EXPAND
ENGAGE

ELEVATE YOUR BRAND, EXPAND YOUR NETWORK, AND ENGAGE YOUR MOST POWERFUL RELATIONSHIPS

JUDI RADICE HAYS

Unstoppable CEO Press

Judi Radice Hays
judi@judihays.com
judihays.com

Elevate, Expand, Engage Judi Radice Hays —1st ed.

ISBN 978-1-955242-07-3

Bulk discounts are available to use as promotions or for corporate LinkedIn and social selling training programs.

For details email: judi@judihays.com

This book is also available in electronic format. Please visit https://judihays.com/bookupdate for details.

CONTENTS

Dedication

My mom's trademark words were "Do Something Nice For Someone Today". This book is for you Mom!

Get Free Updates!

LinkedIn is always changing...stay up to date!

Go to judihays.com/bookupdate right now to get notified
when I release updated content for the book!

Introduction

The worldwide pandemic has changed business in many significant ways. In-person networking events became few and far between - if at all - due to crowd size limitations and social distancing guidelines. Large-scale conferences and trade show gatherings were postponed, and some events went virtual and may stay virtual permanently. Zoom, Teams, Slack, and other communication and video conferencing platforms became widely accepted as a way to conduct business.

The business networking paradigm has shifted due to the pandemic, and some online business practices are not going back to the way they once were.

Most of the ways we used to rely on to meet potential clients, prospect for new business, expand our professional network, and grow our influence, have changed.

According to LinkedIn State of Sales Report 2021,[1] since the start of the pandemic, sellers, who can no longer prospect at in-person conferences and events, are boosting their reliance on

---

[1] https://www.linkedin.com/business/sales/blog/trends/the-linkedin-state-of-sales-report-2021

LinkedIn. Almost three-quarters of B2B sellers (74%)[2] say they committed to expanding their LinkedIn network in 2021. That's great news!

Disruption in the business world has led to innovation, and that is certainly true on LinkedIn.

Such innovation means that LinkedIn plays a vital role for businesses. People are receptive to virtual equivalents in comparison to what used to take place face-to-face. Virtual events such as networking events, conventions, trade shows, business development conversations, sales presentations, video calls, and more are now finding the need to master "digital-first" relationship building skills.

Even once companies bring their teams back in the office and business travel eventually resumes to levels before March 2020, there will still be a case for doing business virtually. It's now more the norm than the exception.

Given the sheer number of global members on LinkedIn, shockingly, only about 1% of users[3] actively post, comment, and otherwise participate in the network weekly, although 91% of marketing executives use LinkedIn as a content source. So, when *you* are active, you'll stand out from the crowd and get noticed.

The more active members become, the more noise there will be in the feed and inboxes – all the more reason to put in the effort now to carve out your visibility!

---

[2]   https://business.linkedin.com/content/dam/me/business/en-us/ sales-solutions/cx/21/pdfs/state-of-sales-report-2021.pdf

[3]   https://www.businessofapps.com/data/linkedin-statistics/

The overall quality of the LinkedIn professional network[4] is indisputable.

As a business owner, you're burning both ends of the candle: running your business while servicing your clients. Your time is limited. You may feel that you can't add LinkedIn to an already full plate. And even if you could, you're not sure what to do with it.

You see others, including your competitors, on LinkedIn publishing, posting, commenting, and showing up in your newsfeed often. You sense there is an opportunity. Are you missing out?

In this book, I will be sharing my proven method of how you can make LinkedIn a valuable weapon in your marketing arsenal. You will learn how to grow your business using the Triple-E Method™ and be given the tools to overcome the biggest challenges in online networking today.

Along the way, I will share my story and my clients' journeys so you can see that this method can and does work consistently - no matter where you are starting today.

You don't have to follow this book in chapter sequence. Dive in wherever you need the help. Each section is organized within the Triple-E Method™.

---

[4]   https://www.businessofapps.com/Edata/linkedin-statistics/

Beginning each section, you will find an overview of that part of the methodology. Following the overview is a description of what to expect in each chapter to help you navigate throughout.

Each chapter ends with an action item checklist.

While this book covers a lot, no one book could address all there is to know about LinkedIn! Throughout this book, I will be referring to my online resources, which provide more information, resources, and training. You can access all the resources at www.judihays.com/bookupdate.

Putting LinkedIn To Work In Your Business

Business executives have some unique challenges to overcome on the path to profitability. You know that just getting your foot in the door with potential clients is tough. Once you find them, it's hard to get the attention of decision-makers. If you have picked up this book, it is probably because you are facing one of these common challenges:

- You struggle with marketing and/or sales strategies to keep your pipeline full
- You endeavor to differentiate yourself from the competition
- You work to grow your business to the next level
- You wrestle with knowing how to use LinkedIn to generate leads

I am here to tell you - the struggle is real! It is not just you. These are things that almost every business leader I know has experienced at one point in time or another. But there is good news - there is a solution, and it's a social network called LinkedIn.

The Evolution Of Linkedin

It's helpful to understand the origins of LinkedIn and how it came about to where it is today as the world's largest B2B virtual networking platform for business professionals.

The mission of LinkedIn is simple: connect the world's professionals to make them more productive and successful.

At its core, LinkedIn is a business and employment-oriented online platform that operates via websites and mobile apps. As a result, it is the single best online resource for virtual business-to-business networking and relationship building with decision-makers, senior-level influencers, opinion leaders, C-level executives, and other industry mavericks, particularly service providers.

Reid Hoffman originally launched the site on May 5, 2003[5] making it older than the other mainstream platforms - Facebook, Twitter and YouTube.

In 2015, most of the company's revenue came from selling subscription access to information about its members to recruiters (Talent Solutions) and sales professionals (Sales Navigator). Around that time, people started using the robust database as a lead generation resource for researching and finding key executives.

Microsoft paid $26 billion to acquire LinkedIn in December 2016 as a wholly owned subsidiary. As of 2017, 94% of B2B marketers used LinkedIn to distribute content.

---

[5]   https://thelinkedinman.com/history-linkedin/

At its core, the platform is designed to be used for professional networking. It started as a way to allow employers to post jobs and for job seekers to find and apply for job openings. As it has grown and matured over the past 18 years. LinkedIn is also now widely used to identify business development opportunities.

As of LinkedIn's Earnings Release FY21 Q4, LinkedIn reported 774+ million registered members from 200 countries and territories.[6]

LinkedIn has seen significant growth on its platform, with content shared up 50% year-over-year in 2020, and record-high levels of engagement reported in FY21 Q2 update[7] from parent company Microsoft. LinkedIn generated $8 billion in revenue in 2020, an increase of 19% year-on-year.

The big transition happening now is the move to being a content creation platform, and the LinkedIn algorithm rewards content creators with news feed visibility.

If you've been using LinkedIn for a while, learning how to make the most of these new opportunities and features can significantly increase your return on the time you invest on this platform.

---

[6] https://www.microsoft.com/en-us/Investor/earnings/FY-2021-Q4/press-release-webcast

[7] https://view.officeapps.live.com/op/view.aspx?src=https://c.s-microsoft.com/en-us/CMSFiles/PressReleaseFY21_Q2.docx?version=b9034409-e6f6-3fbb-129c-3fe9fd1203a8

What's So Special About Linkedin?

Well, for starters, LinkedIn was voted the most trusted social network in 2019[8] by Business Insider. (For the record – Facebook finished last.) According to Hubspot,[9] LinkedIn is 277% more effective at generating B2B leads than Facebook or Twitter.

LinkedIn is where the greatest number of business professionals gather to connect and stay informed, advance their professional aspirations, and work smarter. This undisputable online social platform connects the world's professionals, particularly decision-makers, who can help grow your business!

In the world of business, reputations and relationships matter a great deal. People are so bombarded with messaging and interruptions; they've become numb to the point where they tune out irrelevant or promotional messages.

However, they do want to engage with people and companies who focus on sharing helpful information and relevant content. The people who share useful content that informs and educates aren't simply selling – they're building credible relationships.

Who Should Read This Book?

This book is ideal for top-performing executives and business owners who are serious about building their professional brand on LinkedIn through their personal profile and Company page.

---

[8]   https://business.linkedin.com/marketing-solutions/
corporate-reputation/5-reasons-why-linkedin-is-a-trusted-platform

[9]   https://blog.hubspot.com/blog/tabid/6307/bid/30030/LinkedIn-277-More-Effective-for-Lead-Generation-Than-Facebook-Twitter-New-Data.aspx

The information contained within this book pertains to the leadership of B2B professional service companies wanting to better leverage LinkedIn to increase their brand visibility, thought leadership credibility, and social selling opportunities.

Business development professionals and sales teams who want the knowledge to effectively leverage LinkedIn to identify opportunities, engage in insightful conversations, and generate qualified new business leads will also find this book useful.

Senior-level executives who are changing careers or seeking a job change will also benefit from the fundamental principles to elevate their visibility amongst prospective employers.

The Triple-E Method™

This book is designed to take you from complete novice to feeling confident in your LinkedIn experience. You will start seeing real results if you commit to acting on what you learn. I am excited to be a part of the journey with you!

We will accomplish this through my unique Triple-E Method™

    Elevate - Designing an attractive profile
    Expand - Building your network
    Engage - Creating genuine relationships and earning trust

If you are like me and prefer imagery to visualizing abstract concepts, then you will appreciate this.

Close your eyes and picture a three-legged stool.

Now, think of each of the E's from Triple-E Method™ as a leg to balance the stool. The part you sit on is the Strategy and the three legs need to be balanced to support you (the strategy).

The strategy without the legs is a flat, useless disk. The legs without a strategy have nothing to adhere to. All three legs must be balanced, or you will fall over - or at the very least be doing a lot more work than necessary to stay upright!

Having balance allows you to have a productive marketing campaign for generating increased visibility amongst your prospects. This, in turn, will activate more conversations that result in proposals and closed deals, as well as referrals.

Important to note - your LinkedIn efforts are not a "one and done" profile touch-up or messaging strategy. This method is a system you can put to work in an ongoing way. It allows you to grow consistently and improve over time. It is a strategy that adjusts as your goals and needs do - and even as the platform itself changes.

The Triple-E Method™

Elevate - You ELEVATE by delighting, educating, and informing your audience with the type of content you share. To be found, you must be visible, and you do this through your profile and engaging with meaningful content.

Expand - Next, EXPAND your network - use LinkedIn targeting filters to find the right people you want to connect with. Also, use content strategically to identify interest. There are more opportunities to grow a quality network than you may realize!

Engage – Then, ENGAGE and reach out to grow meaningful relationships within your network. Whether it's inviting someone to connect, leaving a comment, or sending a direct message, this is where the trees bear fruit.

In each section, we will dive into these three areas in more depth. But remember – all the components of this strategy weave together. What you do to **Elevate** your personal brand ties directly to the effort you put into your work to **Engage** with your ideal audience. When you **Expand,** you also **Elevate** your business. It all works together.

Does that seem like a lot to manage?

Don't worry; the Triple-E Method™ serves as a mental hack that helps you remember and implement your LinkedIn strategy in the most effective and seamless way possible. And you will have fun while doing it!

Why I Developed The Triple-E Method™

As a LinkedIn Marketing Strategist and Trainer, what I teach is scalable, obtainable, and effective in generating a substantial return on investment. But the truth is there are no sustainable shortcuts to building credibility. Sure, there are hacks out there that promise you tons of leads or a cheap way to automate your LinkedIn activities through bots and browser plugins. But I must warn you. Those types of shortcuts risk getting your account suspended. LinkedIn takes no prisoners when it comes to adhering to their Terms of Service and User Agreement. Those "get rich quick schemes" are exactly that – schemes – and not worth it. Trust me, I've seen people have their accounts suspended. It's not fun.

LinkedIn is a long game. The more you put into it, the more you get out of it.

When I coach my clients, I demonstrate how they can engage and convert opportunities into meaningful conversations that lead to consistent business growth. I help uncover opportunities that position them as thought leaders in their particular niche.

But when I got started on LinkedIn in 2008, I was like everyone else who starts something new - I had no idea what I was doing. And it was a very different platform back then.

Early in my marketing career, I learned and mastered the nuances of direct response marketing (testing offers, A/B splits, micro-targeting, personalization, etc.). This foundation has evolved into the methodology I use to approach LinkedIn today for myself and my clients.

As VP of Communications for the Austin Chamber of Commerce, I had the unique opportunity to connect on LinkedIn with our member companies. In addition, I led workshops that taught them how they could leverage the power of LinkedIn to build their businesses. This experience first alerted me to how much I enjoy using LinkedIn and teaching others how to make the most of it.

In 2015, when I launched my marketing consultancy, I naturally specialized in LinkedIn. At first, I labeled myself as a "marketing consultant" but found so many of the same type that it was difficult to stand out. Claiming the deeply focused niche into LinkedIn strategy made all the difference.

So, if you are resisting the concept of claiming your niche because you are afraid to miss out on other opportunities, hear me when I say that claiming a niche will allow you to charge a premium. It will also put you in a position of specialization that naturally makes you stand out from the noise.

I spend on average 35 or more hours a week using the platform for myself and on behalf of my clients. And no, you don't need to spend that much time to make it effective for you. I simply share that number to help you understand I actually DO what I teach. I have made it a priority to stay current on the latest changes and newest enhancements on LinkedIn for the benefit of my audience.

That brings us to my purpose for writing this book. It's to help business executives like you overcome fear and get started on this wild ride. Whether a complete newbie, or you dabble around the network, this book helps take you to your next level.

But Does It Work?

The short answer is yes. But don't take my word for it. Throughout this book, I share case studies and examples of this method at work in the real world.

I have seen this method work across various industries, at every level of business from small businesses to multi-million-dollar companies, and with very different personalities.

The bottom line is that this can work for you, too – if you are willing to take the time. This book will provide a guide along the way so that you can take action on LinkedIn efficiently.

PART ONE

ELEVATE

If you provide professional services to other businesses, LinkedIn should be part of your business development strategy. But LinkedIn is not only limited to service-based business - any business that serves other companies (B2B) that needs to find clients, partners, or employees, will find LinkedIn a valuable resource to accomplish those goals.

You hear about the real – and powerful – potential LinkedIn offers to grow your business, but you don't exactly know how the platform works. Where do you start… or even go to find out what LinkedIn can do for you?

What will people think about you? How will they perceive you? Are you worried about saying the wrong thing or looking bad? Feeling imposter syndrome?

Most people starting out on LinkedIn for business development lack the confidence and knowledge about how the platform works and how to use it effectively. Some people have LinkedIn profiles that were created years ago but haven't done anything since. Some people only use LinkedIn when they have a career change.

Many who could benefit most from LinkedIn have no idea how to set up an effective customer-focused profile or use its tools and tremendous reach to build profitable relationships with potential clients and existing connections.

According to marketing software company Moz, LinkedIn scores an almost perfect 100 on its domain authority ranking[10] (an indicator of website credibility).

Why does this matter?

When someone searches your name or business on a search engine, your LinkedIn profile and LinkedIn Company page are likely to be the first, second or third result, sometimes even before your website – it's that important.

ACTION: Just for fun, type your name "first name last name" using quotations in a search engine. See what comes up.

Pro TIP: Create Google Alerts[11] for your name, your company, your clients with their names, companies, and industry news to be alerted when something is indexed in cybersphere.

---

[10]   https://moz.com/domain-analysis/linkedin.com
[11]   https://support.google.com/websearch/answer/4815696?hl=en

The key to success on LinkedIn is to start with a strategy. A game plan. A goal. The first question I ask my client is, "What do you want to accomplish on LinkedIn?"

Then I probe beyond their typical response of, "I want leads." Everyone wants leads. But LinkedIn is a relationship building platform. You need to approach it with a strategy.

Ideally, your strategy should align with your overall business goals and be as specific as possible. Some find it helpful to use the SMART[12] methodology.

This first section will hit on all the critical components of elevating your brand on LinkedIn. And it is as easy as A, B, C.

Amplifying Your Profile

Your profile is the central representation of who you are to the world. As such, we will focus on "above the fold" elements of your profile and maximizing each part. Once you understand what is going on "under the hood," it will be easier to keep this up to date on an ongoing basis and easily pivot along with the normal changes in your business.

Building Your Credibility

Are you using social proof to open doors? Are you making rookie mistakes in how you present your experience or business? You will learn the steps to solve each of these problems in your overall presence on the platform.

---

[12]   https://www.mindtools.com/pages/main/newMN_STR.htm

Creating Your Content

News alert – LinkedIn has evolved into a content-focused platform. Without creating and curating insightful and educational content, you will not be visible in the news feed or to your network. If creating content scares the heck out of you, fear not. You will learn tips to make this easier and take less time while still getting results.

Amplifying Your Profile

Remember that 3-legged stool image? The first leg is the first RE - ELEVATE. It starts with your Profile. Nothing else about your strategy will be successful without a high-impact profile. After all, this is the first thing most people will see when they virtually meet you.

Throughout this chapter I am going to walk you through step-by-step how to make your profile shine. With one caveat - this is not something you only need to do once. Your LinkedIn profile is dynamic and a "living" document that you should continuously update.

Before you do anything else, stop and put two dates on your calendar six months apart. It is okay to stop reading for a minute to open your calendar. These are the days you will review your profile using this chapter to ensure you are on track. Some things to look for:

- Is all the information current, and do the links all work?
- Is your contact information up to date?
- Does your profile photo represent who you are now?
- Are there changes to your audience or strategy that will affect your headline?

- Do you have new things to add to your About section that will set you apart?
- Are there training or certifications you can add?
- How recent are your recommendations?

Ideally, you will make these changes as they happen, but just like you need to schedule a regular oil change on your vehicle (even if it isn't having "problems"), you need to schedule regular maintenance on your LinkedIn profile.

A well-constructed, customer-facing profile is the foundation of all your work to connect with LinkedIn prospects. It takes some effort but pays off in showcasing how you can help clients with your uniqueness.

Profile Myth - It's Not About You

This might surprise you, but... your LinkedIn profile really is not about *you*.

Think of it like this. Your resume is akin to looking in the rearview mirror (to continue with the car analogies). It's all about what you've done, where you've come from. It's factual.

Close your eyes and visualize your LinkedIn profile as your windshield. It's the view of the horizon - the road ahead. It's aspirational. It's how you *want* to be perceived.

Early in my career, a savvy Account Director gave me sage advice to "dress the part." Meaning that I would be the logical choice when an opportunity came up, since I already looked like I belonged in that role. Keeping this in mind, I was promoted regularly to eventually leading the new business development team.

If you approach LinkedIn like this, you will be more likely to attract your prospects. Make them curious and give them a reason to want to connect with you.

One of the silver linings of the pandemic is that professionals fully embraced LinkedIn. In March of 2020, the business world had a reckoning. Business travel came to a halt. In-person meetings and networking quickly pivoted to video meetings. LinkedIn activity skyrocketed. And my LinkedIn marketing consultancy was in such high demand that I was turning away business.

If you were already established on LinkedIn, you were in a great position to benefit. But suddenly, people realized they needed to embrace the platform if they wanted to remain relevant to their customers and prospects. That sparked the idea to write this book. And here we are!

> *82% of buyers are more likely to consider a brand if the person engaging has an informative LinkedIn profile.*[13]

Microsoft's FY21 Q1[14] report revealed that the professional social network saw record levels of engagement in the most recent quarter - up 31%, and a bump in revenue up 16%, driven mainly by increased ad spending. In addition, the report stated, *"Demand on LinkedIn returned to near pre-COVID levels, up 40% year over year, as marketers use our tools to connect with professionals ready to do business."*

---

[13]   https://www.linkedin.com/business/sales/blog/strategy/
six-resources-to-sharpen-virtual-selling-skills

[14]   https://www.microsoft.com/en-us/Investor/earnings/FY-2021-Q1

It is worth clarifying that LinkedIn 'members' and 'active users' are not the same things – LinkedIn doesn't share monthly or daily active user counts, which makes it difficult to gauge the actual comparative usage of the platform.

The bottom line is that LinkedIn was, and still is, the undisputed virtual networking platform for business professionals. It's a rich digital Rolodex[15] of unlimited potential business connections.

So how do you stand out in a crowded space of over 774+ million professionals?

Think of your profile as your canvas. Make it compelling enough to attract traffic. It must resonate with the person reading it and make them curious enough to think, "Wow, I want to know more about this person because it looks like they really understand me and my business."

Suppose your business provides a professional commodity service (such as IT, legal, accounting, recruiting, etc.). If you don't distinguish yourself, it becomes more difficult to attract ideal prospects, and you compete on price rather than on uniqueness of expertise. With all the noise on the platform, you may just get overlooked because your profile lacked a point of differentiation.

For your profile to be an effective marketing promotion tool, it can't be about YOU. Let me repeat that. It's NOT about YOU! It's about what you can do for your audience.

Still not convinced?

---

[15]   https://en.wikipedia.org/wiki/Rolodex

Your LinkedIn profile is a digital first impression.

Eight seconds.

It's not very long, but it's the average length of the human attention span,[16] and it's on a decline. That's how much time you have on LinkedIn to make a positive impression on someone who has never met you before. Ask yourself:

- Is your profile enticing the reader, so that they want to know more about you?
- Does it capture their interest?
- Does it make them curious?
- Does it address their needs?
- Are you capturing enough interest that they want to connect or read more?

Incomplete profiles, or ones that read like a boring resume, are a massive missed opportunity. Instead, strive for a complete and optimized profile that makes the reader curious to want to learn more.

After all, you only have one chance to make a great first impression.

Who Is Your Target Audience?

So, if it's not about you - then who is it about?

Does your profile have curb appeal? Is your profile inviting and providing insights for your audience?

---

[16] https://griffonwebstudios.com/mobile-friendly-website-boost-user-enagement/human-vs-goldfish-attention-span-research/

A bare-bones profile is like an empty restaurant at peak dinner time. When you encounter that, you will most likely keep walking.

An interesting profile speaks directly to your target audience.[17] It should provide insights and engage readers to draw them in effectively - because there's something in it for them, and it's enjoyable to read.

Presenting a customer-focused presence on LinkedIn is akin to having a conversation with your prospects before you ever speak to them. Show that you understand the challenges your target audience faces by educating them. They may not know they have a problem yet. It's up to you to educate them.

Don't talk about yourself or use sales-pitchy language about your offerings touting your solution - instead, lead your reader TO your solution[18] with insightful knowledge that demonstrates your understanding of your audience. You are the subject matter expert, and ultimately, once you build credibility and trust, you earn the right to become a trusted advisor.

> **Pro TIP:** Having trouble determining if your profile is customer-focused? Look at the language. Watch out for too many, "I, me, my" and not enough, "you, your, we."

Above the Fold is Gold

Back in the day, newsstands sold newspapers from every corner. They folded the paper in half, only displaying the headline to

---

[17] https://members.linkedin.com/linkedin-creators-resources/find-your-target-audience

[18] https://blog.goconsensus.com/sales/ceb-dont-lead-with-your-solution-lead-to-it

catch the attention of passersby. If it caught their attention, they would stop and purchase a paper. This is how the term "above the fold" came to be. Likewise, websites use the term "above the scroll," noting that most people don't scroll down from what they see on the home page.

Today the same holds true for LinkedIn. If you're fortunate enough to have a prospect visit your profile, make sure it's compelling enough to spark curiosity and get them to stay.

The introduction section of your profile containing your headline, your profile photo, header image, and contact information is the most important. It is the content a viewer sees before they scroll down. It's prime real estate that receives the most attention from your visitors because it's the first thing they see, which is why it should immediately draw readers in.

Your above-the-fold content should get your customer's head bobbing, thinking, "yes, I want to know more."

It is worth repeating - when somebody reads your headline or looks at your profile, you have less than eight seconds for them to determine if they want to connect or engage with you. Most people won't scroll down to look at your complete profile unless they have a genuine interest.

Make people curious about you!

How do you do that? Let's go through each section of your "above the fold" profile one step at a time.

> **Pro TIP:** Download a PDF[19] of your profile before you make changes.

Your Name On Linkedin

What's in a name? This might seem like the most basic part of the profile, but some still trip up here.

The LinkedIn User Agreement[20] clearly states the name fields may only include the first, middle, and last names of your real or preferred professional name, plus your preferred pronouns. Your name on your LinkedIn profile should be what you want to be called. For example, Michael versus Mike or Elizabeth versus Betty. Don't use other characters, apart from a credential like CPA or MBA. Don't stuff the last name field with keywords – that won't help your visibility one bit and it violates the Terms of Service.

> **Pro TIP:** Make use of the Name Pronunciation[21] feature. This allows you to record and display your name pronunciation on your profile. And it gives the listener a chance to hear your voice. Here are some profiles who have made creative use of this feature:

https://www.linkedin.com/in/mari-fukuyama/
https://www.linkedin.com/in/david-officer/
https://www.linkedin.com/in/salmanshah1922/
https://www.linkedin.com/in/phylliskhare/
https://www.linkedin.com/in/lets-talk-growth-data/

---

[19] https://www.linkedin.com/help/linkedin/answer/4281/
save-a-profile-as-a-pdf
[20] https://www.linkedin.com/help/linkedin/answer/28422/
[21] https://www.linkedin.com/help/linkedin/answer/120710

Your Profile Photo

The first step to creating an authentic profile on LinkedIn is to have a professional-looking headshot to help others recognize you.

Nothing cropped from a vacation or family reunion photo. No selfies in your car or bathroom. No pets. No kids. This is not a dating site or Facebook! And definitely do not use a photo from an old job or graduation 20 years ago.

With the powerful cameras at your disposal on smartphones today, there's no reason why you can't have a decent photo. If you cannot access a professional photographer to take a picture of you, use a tripod and the timer feature, or ask a friend. Smile and look directly into the camera, so people can see who you are.

Your headshot photo is the very first step to build credibility on a virtual platform!

Pro TIP: Having a professional photo makes it 14 times[22] more likely that your profile will be viewed, according to research from LinkedIn. So, investing in hiring a photographer is a wise investment in your personal brand.

Is it time to update your photo? Be authentic if you want to be credible. Would someone be able to recognize you from your photo if they met you in person? It's super important the photo in your profile looks like you as you currently look now. If not, time for an update!

---

[22] https://business.linkedin.com/talent-solutions/blog/2014/12/5-tips-for-picking-the-right-linkedin-profile-picture

Your Background Header Image

There is a large horizontal panel[23] that appears behind your profile photo. I'm amazed at how many people leave it blank. This billboard is a valuable piece of free real estate - a canvas ready for your unique brand message.

What mood or message do you want to convey? What story do you want to tell?

Include something specific to your industry or a geographic location. If you've published a book, include it. If you work in real estate in a recognizable geographic area, use an iconic skyline. Or use this space to convey an aspiration with a visually interesting image.

For example, my goal before the pandemic was to do more public speaking. So I created a collage of images of me presenting to groups of people and used that as my header image.

My goal shifted in 2020 to build on the clout of being a member of Forbes Business Council, and so my current header reflects this prestigious credential.

Whatever you decide, don't leave it blank. That is a waste of valuable space. Instead, make it memorable to help you stand out

---

[23]   https://www.linkedin.com/help/linkedin/answer/49960

from the clutter. This may be just the thing that gets someone to stop and read your profile.

Simply put, there's absolutely no reason why anyone should have a generic background.

> **Pro TIP** – Check the view of your banner on mobile devices and a desktop/laptop computer to make sure your profile photo doesn't cover up important information.

Your Headline

The headline is the text right under your profile photo. Don't waste it on the default job title and company name, or stuff it with generic keywords that don't tell the viewer what is special about you. Instead, use this as a headline to convey your unique message. You have 220 characters to work with.

Your profile photo and the first 25 – 45 characters of your headline follow you everywhere on LinkedIn. It shows with all your posts and comments, in search results, in notifications. It weighs heavy in whether people accept your invites. Pay extra close attention to this because it's what could compel someone to click on your profile to find out, "who is this interesting person who looks like someone I want to know more about?" or ignore your outreach.

Here are some examples of headlines:

> *Improving Conversion Rates for a Predictable Pipeline for B2B Services Firms ★ Build Trust and Win More Ideal Clients ★ Reaching The Right People With The Right Messages ★ Podcast Host*

Connecting Suppliers & Retailers in the Creative Arts & Home Decor Industries for Better Access and Increased Sales & Profits | Podcast Host

Helping Pharma, Biologic and Medical Device Companies Optimize Performance and Maximize Opportunities in Federal Markets

Improving the Leadership and Culture of Organizations Through Tailored Training & Coaching on Emotional Intelligence, Resiliency and Well-Being | Certified Master Trainer EQ-i 2.0 and EQ 360 | Keynote Speaker

Creating Powerful Positioning Strategies for Product Marketing Leaders Using a Systematic Framework That Makes it Easier for Buyers to Buy | Expert in B2B Software

Providing B2B Software Companies a Systematic Positioning Framework to Develop Powerful Messages That Build Awareness and Demand for a Competitive Advantage

Transforming the Way Hiring Managers in the Energy Industry Plan and Execute Their Workforce Strategy for Long Term Success | Bridging Business Challenges with Cost-Effective Workforce Solutions

Pro TIP: Stuck on what to include in your headline? Try this formula: Who you serve (your ideal audience) + What you do for them (unique services you provide) + What results you deliver (why they should care). Look at what your competitors or similar profiles are saying so you know the playing field. Use Title Case formatting.

> **For example:**
>
> **"We Help Women Veterinarians Get Their Finances Together So They Can Build Lasting Wealth."**

Given the dynamic nature of LinkedIn, you can easily change your headline. I recommend you review it from time to time to stay relevant depending on your strategy for using LinkedIn.

For example, say you are trying to connect with logistics executives right now because you're offering a new service or technology related to the supply chain industry. Try a new eye-catching headline to see what response you get. If they're not receptive to connecting with you… you can easily change it.

Your Contact Info

Many people overlook this section. Make it easy for people to reach you in the contact info[24] drop-down menu. Include your business website, calendar appointment link, blog or portfolio, Twitter handle, and business email.

I include more than a link to my main website in my contact section. I also include a free worksheet and my online appointment scheduler for free consultation calls.

Consider getting a phone number that is not your personal cell phone. I use a Google Voice number, which screens my calls to cut down on unwanted solicitations. I've also created a unique email address just for LinkedIn. Both strategies allow me to track

---

[24]   https://www.linkedin.com/help/linkedin/answer/34987/
       edit-the-contact-info-section-of-your-profile

outreach from LinkedIn and quickly identify any spammers who add me to email funnels without my permission.

Give the reader multiple ways to engage with you.

> **Pro TIP:** You can see exactly when you connected with someone by looking at their contact info box.

The Featured Section

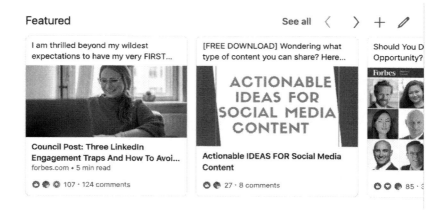

The Featured[25] section allows you to showcase specific content to people who view your LinkedIn profile. Use the Featured section to highlight a recent blog article, links to videos, a slide deck, or whatever you want; two to three items work best. Keep it relevant and interesting.

This eye-catching section is a way to grab attention. Use it to build credibility and let your uniqueness shine through. Update

---

your Featured section often with your best content. Do NOT put your resume here.

The Most Underutilized Section

Guess which part of LinkedIn profiles is underutilized or, worse yet, misused?

It's the About section.

The biggest and most common mistake I see is that people use their About section to talk about themselves. Contrary to the name "About," this section is not about YOU. Remember, your LinkedIn profile is not your resume. The About section should never be written in the third person. Nor should it be a regurgitation of your CV or a bulleted list of your skills/accomplishments.

The About section is actually about your audience - the person who is reading your profile.

The purpose of the About section is to figure out what you can do to spark curiosity. What you say can compel someone to click "see more…" to read the entire entry. The first three lines of your About section are like the subject line of an email. What's your hook? Does it motivate the reader to want to click 'READ MORE"?

Elements Of A Solution-Filled About Section

Approach your About section as if invited to speak at a professional event to an ideal audience of prospective clients. You certainly wouldn't spend the time talking about yourself. That would be a disaster.

Instead, you do your homework and clearly understand the problems and challenges your audience may experience. They have a problem (they might not know they have this problem). You have a solution to their problem, but you will turn them off if you lead with that.

Your job is to educate them to be better informed "buyers" of your service or product.

- What would you talk about that would be of interest to them?
- What insights would you share?
- What do you want them to learn from your talk?

The answers to these questions are what you should include in your About section.

Your About section is where your messaging needs to align with your prospects' business challenges. The better grasp you have on this, the better your ability to speak the language that will resonate with your prospect.

Don't waste this section on a sales pitch or keyword stuffing. That's the quickest way to lose the attention of your audience.

Take the time to gain clarity about your prospect's pain points.

Keenan, author of Gap Selling, underscores the importance of knowing your customer's business inside and out through a series of questions to get to the root cause of their pain. Your customer may be experiencing technical problems, business problems, and/or existential problems. By asking provoking questions in discovery, this will lead to the root cause. If you can confidently identify a problem, show the buyer that you understand its impact on their business, AND articulate the root cause in their industry terms, all leading to your solution to that specific problem, you are as Keenan would say "golden".

Here's an example. My client owns a sales marketing agency that works with home decor manufacturers to help them get their merchandise into big-box retail. His About section leads with the "pain" his target audience faces:

> *"Without a cohesive strategy for bringing products to market, manufacturers' sales would be flat or decline, and their relationships with retailers would be weaker. The problems we see commonly with vendors and manufacturers... see more*

This opening resonates with his prospect audience and they are likely to click "see more".

Use the allocated 2000 characters to show your subject matter expertise and whatever you want to be known for by providing the reader with something of value. Make sure you address your reader using *"you, you're, we,"* not *"I, me, my."*

Employ a paradigm shift to change how your prospects think about their business in a way that leads back to your unique differentiator.

True differentiators are not:

- Features and benefits common in your market
- Vague or overused descriptions
- Sales pitches

The key to real insight isn't a story about your solution at all. It's a story about your prospect and how they've missed something materially important to their business performance. Demonstrate the outcomes that your product generates for them to relieve their pain.

Provide advice, tips, and insights. Do it in a way that comes across to whoever's reading your About section, that you're giving them some useful information. You're identifying their problem and letting them know you have the solution to relieve their pain.

Don't sell. Instead educate.

Nobody cares for the guy at the party who can only talk about how great he is. He might be amazing, but we hate hearing it directly from him. Likewise, leading with your solution compromises credibility. Your buyer will naturally gravitate towards your specific solution if you can frame the value of your solution's differentiators as being the only way to fulfill the outcomes needed by their business.

At the end of the About section, you may add a "call to action" to invite them to have a conversation. No strings attached. And let them know no matter what, you will provide something that can benefit them, like:

- Informative content that leads to your solution
- Starting with the challenge your target prospect faces
- Explaining the pain/problem that you solve
- Offering helpful tips and insights
- Adding a call-to-action

Pro TIP: The first three lines of your About section must be compelling enough to get the reader to click on "...see more".

Here are more examples of customer focused About sections from several of my client's profiles:

https://www.linkedin.com/in/susantatum/
https://www.linkedin.com/in/lawsonabinanti/
https://www.linkedin.com/in/clint-orear/
https://www.linkedin.com/in/victorquaye/
https://www.linkedin.com/in/oresteapetillo/
https://www.linkedin.com/in/mari-fukuyama/
https://www.linkedin.com/in/kevin-ruda/

Check out the first part of my About section and how I've focused on my prospect's pain:

About

▶ It is critical today, in order to stand out from the crowded marketplace, that YOU and your company brand show your uniqueness like nobody else. It starts with having a strategy to create compelling content that gets visibility with your target audience. Your content has to be something that THEY find relevant. That's a tall order if you are busy running a business.

Clients come to me because they lack visibility on LinkedIn and they also realize they are missing out on a huge opportunity. Turning that around with magnetic content strategies to make them visible experts is where I do my best work. I take that off your plate so you can focus on what you do best - run your company!

▶ **3 LinkedIn Strategies that you can implement NOW**

❶ Reorient your LinkedIn profile from a you-focus to a customer-focus. Include bits of VALUE and disruptive perspectives that your ideal prospects can immediately put to use.

❷ Grow your network strategically. Use Boolean strings to run targeted searches and personalize each invite. VISIT the profiles of your ideal customers. Many of them will view back and invite you to connect with them. TIP: Always send a welcome message - never SELL!!!

❸ Use your Notifications to engage with your connections - like, share, and comment on their posts. Encourage them with endorsements; thank them; offer follow-up resources; PROMOTE them!

BONUS TIP: When was the last time you downloaded your database of connections? There are diamonds in the rough to be discovered. Sort by Job Title or Company or Keyword and reach out with a direct message. You'll be amazed at the results

My services include LinkedIn content strategies, white-glove LinkedIn account management & marketing strategy, content creation, email campaigns, website maintenance, and other B2B marketing services with a focus on engaging audiences to start more qualified conversations.

Expertise with professionals in B2B companies, who sell high ticket services, and who are willing to invest time in learning how to leverage the power of inbound marketing to generate leads and become visible experts, all so they can grow their business.

 If you're ready to tap into the power of inbound marketing to grow your business and engage with prospective buyers, let's chat. I'll provide insights you can use right away.

In the next chapter we examine "below the fold" sections of your profile and how to build your credibility. Once able to optimize these sections, you will be on your way to attracting your ideal clients.

Action Items:

- ☐ Focus your profile on your target audience and their needs
- ☐ Have a profile photo that is professional, recent, and authentic
- ☐ Complete all the sections of your profile
- ☐ Make use of the banner image
- ☐ Write a compelling headline to convey your unique value proposition
- ☐ Keep your contact information current
- ☐ Spend time on writing a solution filled About section that is informative and educational

Building Your Credibility

Over the years, as an avid LinkedIn user, I have developed, refined, and perfected a unique method that will take your LinkedIn experience from boring to blazing. Following the methodology and tracking your progress, you will start making relationships that matter. And your business will grow as a result.

Having an effective "above the fold" profile will start producing immediate results in the way people see you, but clients and potential clients that keep scrolling are invested! They are looking for something more - and you have the opportunity to give it to them.

The Activity Section

Did you know that 22% of users in the US visit LinkedIn daily?[26] "Visit" is the operative word here. A high degree of visitors are merely observing, not actively engaging.

The activity section is one of the first things to look at when visiting a profile. It shows what the person has been up to on LinkedIn in articles, posts, comments, and reactions. By looking

---

[26]   https://www.statista.com/statistics/815162/
frequency-with-which-us-internet-users-visit-linkedin/

at this, you can find out what is important to this person, and if it makes sense, you can engage with them.

Another interesting thing is that you can see the number of followers (which generally correlate to the number of connections) by looking at someone's activity section.

Engaging with their content is a great way to warm up a prospect before inviting them to connect. They get a notification of your action. You've now become visible to them. This notification may even prompt them to visit your profile. So when you reach out to connect, your invite is more likely to be accepted because they recognize you've shown interest in their content.

> **Pro TIP:** Want to keep your high-value prospects top of mind? Create a folder or bookmark of the activity feeds of your top 10 prospects. Spend 15 minutes daily reviewing their feeds and engage accordingly.

We will go in-depth into creating your content and how to engage with others' content in future chapters.

The Experience Section

Experience doesn't matter as much if you use LinkedIn for business development versus looking for a job. But either way, LinkedIn is not a clone of your resume. You don't have to list all your responsibilities at past jobs or anything like that. Nobody cares. (Sorry!). Keep it short and focused. It's totally acceptable not to have any description. That's what your resume is for.

Another common mistake I see here is that people have the generic, gray square avatar to the left of an entry because it is not connected to a company page, entity, educational institution, volunteer non-profits, etc., on LinkedIn. To the viewer, those gray avatars make your profile look incomplete and a bit sketchy. This happens for a variety of reasons:

- The organization is no longer in business
- The organization doesn't have a company page
- There is an organization page, but it's not properly connected to the profile
- The organization created a personal profile instead of a Company page
- You own your business but haven't created a Company page yet
- You are self-employed, contract working, or in between jobs, and not connected to any particular organization

Do a quick check that your previous experience and education connect correctly to the official company pages on LinkedIn. If you see the gray avatar, be sure to find the correct page to connect to.

> **Pro TIP:** Add your various services or progressive growth in your company experience description using the position grouping feature in your profile's Experience Section[27]

---

[27]   https://www.linkedin.com/help/linkedin/answer/94894/

Company Pages

According to Statista,[28] there are over 57 million business profiles (Company pages) on LinkedIn. Yet, if I had a buck for all the profiles of business owners, consultants, and entrepreneurs who haven't created their free Company page, I'd be retired on an island sipping a fancy drink with a tiny umbrella.

Business owners who have not created their free Company page[29] are missing out on a huge opportunity. For one, it makes their business look credible. Secondly, it doubles the opportunity for your content to show up in the feed. Thirdly, all LinkedIn pages are indexed on search engines, so no Company page means you're not showing in the results - but your competitor is!

If you own your own company, are self-employed, taking contract work or in between jobs, creating a company page[30] is easier than you think, and best of all, it's free. Come up with a name, create a logo, fill out the profile...the works.

Fully completed pages get 30% more weekly views. It not only validates your business, but your competition often overlooks it. And it is indexed in search engines provided you've optimized all the settings. There's nothing worse than seeing a barren Company page with no content and a handful of followers. It's like an abandoned building.

---

[28] https://www.businessofapps.com/data/linkedin-statistics/
[29] https://www.linkedin.com/help/linkedin/answer/100826
[30] https://business.linkedin.com/marketing-solutions/linkedin-pages/best-practices

Company Page Power Tips

- Make use of all the Company page features
- Develop a content strategy to showcase your brand
- Consistently invite your connections to follow your Company page
- If you have a team, empower them to invite connections to follow the page
- Expand your visibility with brand ambassadors sharing content from the page
- Showcase your company culture spotlighting your team
- Create and maintain Showcase pages
- Systemize & simplify activities, so that everyone can participate
- Publish articles as your Company page
- Regularly share company updates and news
- Post open jobs and connect with potential employees
- Recruit prospective employees
- Build a community by encouraging your team to engage with the content
- Customize your call-to-action button to align with your goals
- Add a follow button to your website and email signature
- Respond to every comment on your posts (when warranted)
- Track growth and engagement with robust built-in reporting

When you have both an active personal profile and Company page, you become even more visible. You have more opportunities to show up in search engine results. Companies that post weekly see a 2x lift in engagement[31] with their content.

You can grow your Company page followers by following best practices.[32] Once a Page has 150+ followers, the opportunity for growth becomes exponential; 500+ followers opens up additional features.

Visibility is a product of your activity on LinkedIn. And since LinkedIn is indexed in search engines as a highly authoritative domain, the greater your opportunity will be for you and your company to show up in search results.

Don't let connecting to Company pages be an afterthought. Having an optimized Company page will help you show up in searches on LinkedIn; it's for enhanced visibility.

Building Social Proof To Form Your Credibility

Social proof, based on the idea of normative social influence[33], is the influence of other people that leads us to conform in order to be liked and accepted by them and it is the lifeblood of any business. And LinkedIn is a great way to build up a stock of recommendations and glowing words from people you've worked with, past clients, and others. But don't let all that praise stay on LinkedIn. Be sure to download your data files regularly.

---

[31]   https://www.qualtrics.com/blog/online-review-stats/
[32]   https://business.linkedin.com/marketing-solutions/linkedin-pages/for-small-business
[33]   https://en.wikipedia.org/wiki/Normative_social_influence

On LinkedIn, there are two major types of social proof - Skill Endorsements and Recommendations. Each one is important for different reasons.

The Skill Endorsements Section

This section is confusing to many people. Skills are essentially keywords that the recruiting Talent Solutions platform uses when matching employees to job openings. It's wise to use all 50 slots for an optimized profile - but only list skills that are important and consistent with your current or future business strategy. Generic skills are meaningless to your target audience.

According to LinkedIn, people who list at least five skills receive up to 17x more profile views. The more endorsements you have for your skills, the higher you'll rank in the search results.

Endorsing one of your connections for an obvious skill is not disingenuous. When used as a gesture of kindness, endorsements are a great way to get their attention - like a gentle tap on the shoulder. They'll get a notification that you endorsed them, and two out of three times, they'll reciprocate or send you a message acknowledging it. This is an easy way of building credibility to nurture your network. It may even spark a conversation.

You can select the top three skills to have featured in your profile. Strive to get 99+ endorsements for each!

The Recommendations Section

Walt Whitman once said, "If you did it, it ain't bragging." So if someone else says kind words about what you've done in the form of a recommendation, that goes a long way!

While skill endorsements are helpful, particularly for job seekers, full-on recommendations[34] are much more powerful. Testimonials are the highest level of social proof and are vitally important in building trust. From a prospecting point of view, recommendations provide helpful information and insights you can use when sending invitations to connect. Reading what people write about others will give you a glimpse into the person.

Opportunities to ask for recommendations in a non-intrusive way happen all the time if we look for them. Let's say you facilitate a webinar or something similar where there is an audience. Send out a survey afterward asking for feedback. Review the feedback, and if you find a few quotes that speak to your knowledge, etc., reach out and thank whoever paid a compliment. Ask them if you could include their feedback on your LinkedIn profile and to make it easy for them, copy and paste what they wrote, and request it from LinkedIn. In return, you could offer them a copy of your slide presentation or handout as an incentive.

Aim for an approximate 3:2 ratio[35] of recommendations received versus given. People who receive AND give recommendations appear to be actively engaged LinkedIn members.

Try not to request multiple recommendations on the same day. Recommendations with the same date could look suspect. Instead, have a game plan to reach out to a couple of people regularly, at least once a month.

---

[34] https://www.linkedin.com/help/linkedin/answer/90

[35] https://www.linkedin.com/posts/johnespirian_fridayshout-linkedinlearnerlounge-activity-6823541693447450624-u1c9

Think about giving recommendations to others if you feel you've had a positive experience but don't expect one back. Do it because you want to share a random act of kindness. Quid pro quo recommendations are less credible. When you recommend someone, you put your credibility behind that person – it is important that you mean it!

By originating the recommendation on LinkedIn, it stays with your profile. You can then copy the text and add it to your website and other marketing materials.

Claim Your Public Profile URL

Ever see those extra numbers and letters at the end of a LinkedIn web address? That's the default assigned to you when you created your account. Instead, claim your custom URL[36] to make it easier to connect with you.

You can use a variation of your name and/or your professional brand since you'll share this URL with people, so they can find your LinkedIn profile. The customizable part of the URL is not case sensitive, meaning using JohnSmith, johnsmith, or johnSmith will all point to the same profile. Keep in mind that if you do change your profile URL, previous URLs will not work, so update your external links accordingly.

Managing Your Account And Privacy Settings

Get familiar with the numerous Privacy & Settings[37] that allows you to manage your account.

---

[36] https://www.linkedin.com/help/linkedin/answer/87/customize-your-public-profile-url

[37] https://www.linkedin.com/help/linkedin/answer/66

Linkedin And Identity Theft

With the shift to virtual networking, LinkedIn has experienced an influx of people using automation and hackers looking for their next mark. Bad actors use nefarious tools to scrape public data from LinkedIn to find personal information they can use to steal your identity. Be cautious in the detail of personal information you share there. You don't need to include your high school and/or year you graduated, pet's name, personal email, and the like. Keep your confidential information private.

Be selective in the invitations you choose to accept. Always look at the profile of the person asking to connect with you. Look at their activity, the size of their network, and your common connections. If there is no message with the invite, I usually pass on those. Only accept if it meets your LinkedIn network strategy. Don't be swayed by pretty faces. If it looks too good to be true, it probably is a fake profile. In those cases, click Ignore and move on.

> **Pro TIP:** If you encounter one of those suspicious profiles, use Google Reverse Image search to see if the photo is a stock image or stolen from someone else's identity. Add the extension to your browser for easy use.

Use two-step authentication[38] and a very secure password. Also, check the number of active sessions where you are signed in[39] to verify a third party isn't accessing your account without your permission.

---

[38] https://www.linkedin.com/help/linkedin/answer/531
[39] https://www.linkedin.com/help/linkedin/answer/50190

The goal here is not to scare you. Instead, it is to make you aware that some nefarious scammers[40] use LinkedIn, and to help you learn simple tools to protect yourself.

Don't Click That Link

Unfortunately, hackers have figured out LinkedIn is fertile territory. As a rule, do not click any links in messages, even if you KNOW the sender unless you have specifically agreed to receive that link.

I've received weird messages from known connections that contain a link or a PDF to download. But the language in the message was a bit off, or the URL looked odd.

Trust your instinct.

Bad actors on LinkedIn spread malware and compromise accounts. If you accept invitations without vetting them, you risk getting your account hacked and spamming your network. Be cautious.

> **Pro TIP:** It never hurts to ask. If you get a link from a connection unexpectedly, send a quick message or email letting them know the link looks suspicious. This gives them an opportunity to see it and verify it is legitimate.

Also, don't be one of those people who send long, exhaustive, obviously "scripted messages" containing a bunch of links. If you want to send someone a link, always ask permission first. Then

---

[40] https://www.techrepublic.com/article/
data-scraped-from-500-million-linkedin-users-found-for-sale-online/

they will be more receptive to your message. If they say no, you are actually building credibility.

Becoming A Niche Authority

Becoming a niche authority starts by building a profile that demonstrates your expertise, clarifies to the reader what problems you solve, who you solve them for, and how you are unique in the space. Remember to use all the tools at your disposal on your profile and in using LinkedIn in general.

If you have an active Twitter account, connect LinkedIn to it (unless it is a personal account you don't want shared). This way, when you post something, you can automatically share it on your Twitter feed.

LinkedIn Learning (formerly known as Lynda) is another great resource for increasing your knowledge. You can discover, complete, and track courses related to your field and interests. LinkedIn includes Learning with a paid premium subscription. However most public libraries are now offering free access to this resource.

The LinkedIn Skill Assessments feature allows you to demonstrate your knowledge of the skills you've added to your profile by completing assessments specific to those skills, usually 15 multiple-choice questions.

After you have the foundation of a strong profile, you build your authority in your niche on LinkedIn by sharing content that appeals to your target audience. If you are just starting and don't have original content, you can begin by sharing insightful comments on others' posts in your niche. In the next couple of chapters, we will address content more in-depth.

There is a process to creating your presence on LinkedIn. But at some point, if you put in the work, you will start to see consistent opportunities on a steady basis. The measure of success depends on the consistent efforts you put forth.

Getting to this point where people seek you out, especially if you're just starting to become active on LinkedIn, takes time. It's a long game – not a sprint. It takes time to begin seeing tangible results based on your strategy, the goals you've set, and your commitment to attaining those goals.

Action Items:

- [ ] Build a company page if you own your own business or are self-employed
- [ ] Connect your experience to company pages for increased credibility and searchability
- [ ] Invest time into building social proof through recommendations
- [ ] Claim your public profile URL to build your brand
- [ ] Regularly review your account and privacy settings
- [ ] Use best practices to avoid spammers and scammers

Crafting Content That Builds Your Bottom Line

Content is unique in that it is both a part of **Elevating** your brand and your business, **Expanding** your network and building clientele. In this chapter, we will bridge both the purposes of content and give you a good foundation for curating and creating content.

Being a good curator of relevant content [lists, resource guides, best of, etc.] on LinkedIn is also a powerful way to become a subject matter expert. By doing so, you leverage that content without having to be a content creator. However, it's always better if you create your content. That's what gives you more credibility.

Become known as a "go-to" resource in your niche.

The way the LinkedIn algorithm works is that your activity typically shows up in about 10% of your follower's newsfeed. If there is engagement early on (first hours of the post), then the reach has the potential to expand to a wider audience beyond your immediate network. This is also why it's important to grow your network consistently. Otherwise, you are limiting your reach.

Easing Into Your Role As A Content Creator

If you're new to creating content, writing articles, and commenting on social media posts in a business setting, this process can feel understandably intimidating. Consider what is best received by your audience and your comfort level.

Since you've done the research, you are informed about what's relevant and already being discussed. And with a content strategy, you will have a game plan.

Your content will get visibility from your ideal clients by bringing your expertise and knowledge to the newsfeed.

Go From Invisible To Visible

There are a lot of great LinkedIn profiles that never get seen by their intended audience. The profile sits there with no activity – and more importantly, no incoming business offers as a result!

Content is the way you make the transformation on LinkedIn. At first, content creation can be intimidating or even downright overwhelming. You may want to start with observing what your competitors are doing or check out the thought leaders in your industry. What is relevant and trending? What topics are covered?

Observe the type of content getting reactions from your ideal audience. To facilitate this, try bookmarking a handful of active profiles so you can efficiently view their activity feeds. If you find something interesting and want to refer to it in the future, use the SAVE[41] feature. This is one of the best ways to "bookmark" content you want to refer to.

After you've identified what is topical and what is of interest to your audience, make a note:

- Which hashtags are included?
- What format of content is used?
- What types of posts get attention?
- Look at the number of reactions and comments
- Watch whose profiles engage

Now that you feel comfortable with the information you've gathered, go ahead and either comment on a post or create your own. Maybe you share an article you find interesting. When you share it, add a caption mentioning why you like the article or the key takeaways. Be sure the article is not behind a paywall (gated content).

Perhaps you are attending an interesting event or webinar. You can write about or share the key takeaways after the event. You can discuss something you observe as it relates to your business.

Or you could create a poll to survey your audience. The LinkedIn Polls[42] features make it easy for members to engage by asking their opinion about various topics. Polls help you understand trends and can be a great conversation starter. You can publish the results of the survey with your commentary.

---

[41] https://www.linkedin.com/help/linkedin/answer/70754/save-content-in-your-feed

[42] https://www.linkedin.com/help/linkedin/answer/119171

Case Study

One of my clients created a poll about the greatest pain points their target market was experiencing. They predicted they would get one type of response but were surprised by the answers. It gave them valuable insights into what their customers were dealing with in real time.

They then took the information, analyzed the responses in greater detail and wrote a comprehensive article. We created branded graphics showing the results and shared key solutions to each of the biggest pain points. This was shared as an article[43] on their website, and as a series of posts on LinkedIn.

In addition to the content generated, we now had a valid opportunity to reach out to the people who participated in the poll to offer them an analysis of the findings. The results were presented in a professional manner which built their credibility and positioned them as a valuable resource to their ideal client.

Sometimes polls will reveal unexpected details about your clients. These polls help you adjust your overall marketing and approach.

The possibilities are endless. Because you've put in the time to research to see what type of topics and formats your ideal clients express an interest in, and you are clear on the specific problems your clients may be experiencing, you have the ingredients you need to start sharing your own relevant content.

---

[43]   https://jbf-consulting.com/is-shipper-of-choice-dead/

> **Pro TIP:** Start looking at the content you see every day with a more critical eye - what do you like about it or dislike? What draws you in? These insights will help you create better content.

Getting Started With Content Creation

There are a lot of different content strategies and tools to make content creation easier. We will start with the basics first and then dive into some different approaches so that you can find what resonates the most with your business and goals.

Understanding B2B Marketing Media

The lines between media channels can be blurry. Sometimes a piece of content may be published first in a trade magazine, then shared on LinkedIn, and then mentioned on your blog.

Visibility of your thought leadership content can attract influencer engagement, realize potential partnerships, and bring in business opportunities that extend beyond your imagination.

The four types of media are you have access to are:

- Paid media to amplify
- Earned media to earn credibility
- Shared media to distribute
- Owned media is your original content, and you decide where to publish

Earned Media

Earned media is "word of mouth" exposure through things written about you and your company. You can make yourself known to editors and journalists or pitch ideas based on editorial calendars. If there is an interest in your idea, you will have earned media exposure. Not all media coverage is favorable so for this example, we will focus on earning positive media mentions.

Earned media is the free impressions resulting from any non-paid media publicity. This includes mentions earned through content marketing, social reposts/tweets, customer experience (reviews and ratings), and PR/press mentions/publicity efforts. For instance, being invited to appear as a guest on podcasts is earned media exposure.

Getting your name in print from a reputable source lends credibility and increases your visible exposure.

An example of how to get earned media coverage:

- Create a resource list of the top 10 podcasts, in a specific niche relevant to your audience (content curation)
- Publish the resource list on your blog (owned media)
- Share it on your LinkedIn newsfeed (shared social media), making sure to tag the podcast hosts mentioned on the list
- Over a period of time, create posts to highlight specific podcast shows and link back to your main article

Results:

- Your followers engage with your post
- The expanded network of your followers sees the post and the activity
- One of the podcasts listed invites you to be a guest on their show

- The podcast host now promote you on their website
- You share this on your owned media and social media channels
- An industry publication reaches out and offers you a guest column or interview
- The next thing you know, a prospect listens to your podcast interview and reaches out to you for a consultation to help solve a problem that you have a solution for BTW, this is a true story that just happened for one of my clients.

Shared Social Media

Shared media, also known as social media, is driven by user-generated content and algorithms that you have zero control over. The benefit of shared social is that established social platforms already have an audience, so you can leverage that right away.

Companies can make use of social media as a source of communications internally and externally. It includes not just social networking, but community, partnerships, distribution, customer service, chat bots, and promotional content.

There is no "one size fits all," when it comes to shared media. Test what works for your audience. Do not share the same content in the same exact format across different platforms. Each platform has its own size and format requirements, as well as unique audiences.

The most important caveat about shared social is that you cannot control the conversation. If things go sideways, which they sometimes do, you'll need to have a crisis management plan. Don't wait until there is a crisis to have a plan in place.

Owned Media

Owned media is what you have total control over for the most part. It's the original content you create through your company website. Owned media are blogs, case studies, your podcasts, your email campaigns, eBooks, research reports, white papers, etc.).

Since you create the content, you control the messaging, the branded imagery, to tell the story how you want it told. Your original content, your owned media, is all about thought leadership. And thought leadership is about being an authority in your niche. Others see you as an expert … even your competitors.

When creating your original content, build it as one large piece so it can be repurposed into bite-sized pieces that can be shared everywhere. Once you've published your original content, you can repurpose and share it in various forms on the other types of media channels to amplify your message and grow your audience.

The primary goal of original content is to provide informational and educational value to your audience. However, to truly own it, always publish on your website first, index it in Google Search Console and then use the other channels for promotion and distribution. Your email list is also something you own.

The best content strategy is to put effort into building your equity where you own it. Then make use of the built-in audiences on the rented platforms to amplify your message. Sharing your content on LinkedIn is a great way to drive traffic back to your website.

Also, if you create evergreen content (timeless content), it can be re-shared again and again. LinkedIn content that has performed well, when re-shared, continues to perform well.

Paid Media

Paid media is exactly that - it's media that you pay to have delivered to specific audiences. It may include search ads, boosted social media posts, sponsored content, Google AdWords, retargeting, LinkedIn Marketing Solutions, Facebook ads, etc.

On most social platforms, organic reach is hard to attain because of algorithms, so you have to pay to play to boost posts in order to get decent visibility in the newsfeed. Once you start paying, your organic reach will drop considerably. LinkedIn still has fairly good organic reach, but that will eventually change as LinkedIn has profitability goals to reach.

If you primarily provide a professional service to other businesses (B2B), no other platform is as effective as LinkedIn is for B2B targeting. LinkedIn Marketing Solutions offers a paid option, with the ability to micro-target your B2B buyers far better than any other platform. However, you must be willing to invest the budget and produce the content to make the most out of this targeted outreach.

When all four media types are working at their optimal performance, it can help you establish authority and expand your visibility.

Build Your Media Muscle

Sometimes you just need to start! Build your muscles by starting with baby steps, and before you know it, you will run—and if you are lucky enough, you will soar.

Develop your content strategy with this exercise:

The intel gathered in this exercise will inform your content creation strategy:

- Identify your audience persona(s) as specifically as possible
- Hone in on their priorities and pain points - what is their problem that you solve
- Reveal the impacts - what happens to them if that problem isn't solved
- Dig deeper to find the root causes of what really causes the pain
- Create valuable thought leadership content that addresses the causes
- Leverage multiple channels to distribute your content
- Always include a next step – a call to action

Many companies struggle to get their content strategy right. If you take steps to do it well and offer your potential clients exactly what they are looking for—insight and perspective—you will have a tremendous advantage. And when it's time to select a professional service provider, you will likely be at the top of the list.

The Other Payoff From Posting Content

Just as with the Google search algorithm, you train the LinkedIn algorithm to recognize your content as relevant when you post on LinkedIn regularly. The algorithm also factors in how much engagement you have by way of comments, reactions and shares, and how much time people dwell on reading your posts, and more.

Profiles that are active in this way will show up more in search results than dormant profiles.

If content is king, then consistency in posting content is its queen.

Types Of Content Strategies

Getting started, I recommend the same basic steps mentioned in the above exercise. But then there are different ways to approach organizing your content. The steps are:

Create A Content Asset Library

Take an inventory of ALL the content you've published and what's been published about you (this could be blog posts, news articles, videos, podcasts, etc.).

Catalog ALL Your Content On All Platforms

Use a spreadsheet to catalog your content inventory. To get a sample content inventory spreadsheet go to JudiHays.com/bookupdate.

Perform A Content Audit

Track the engagement performance to identify your top-performing content. What are the views, reactions, comments, and reshares? Google Analytics and Search Console can be useful for finding website content metrics.

Identify What Is Evergreen, What Needs Update

Some of your previously published content will need to be updated. Some will stand the test of time. Use your spreadsheet to make note for each piece of content.

Identify The 3 Top Pain Points Of Your Audience

The way to get your audience's attention is to make it relevant to them. This is why it is imperative to be crystal clear about the root causes of the problems that your audience experiences.

Map The Content To The Pain Points

Now you want to review each of your content pieces and identify any of the 3 pain points it addresses. Content may address multiple pain points. And some content will not focus on any pain points. This needs to be noted to see where you may need to create new content.

Slice Up The Most Relevant Content For Social Media Sharing

Start with your long-form articles, eBooks, or podcast/video recordings and break them down into digestible snacks for your audience to feast on.

Experiment With Different Formats

The LinkedIn algorithm loves variety so try different formats and types of content to see which perform best with your audience.

Invite Your Audience To Engage

Start with an end in mind. Tell your reader what you want them to do - make it easy for them. You can ask them a question or request they leave a comment. They don't always do it, but if you don't ask, it's less likely they will engage.

Set Benchmarks And Track Engagement Metrics

This will give you a lens into by whom and how your content is consumed. Also, if content performs well and it's timeless, it can be shared again and again. Later in this book, we take a deeper dive into what to measure.

Pay Attention To WHO Is Engaging

This is the golden nugget! Look at who engages with your content and use it as an opportunity to further the conversation. If you're connected with them, this is an opening for a conversation. Thank them for their participation. If you're not connected, and they match your target personas, now you have the perfect opportunity to invite them to your network. By using content to grow your network strategically, you will increase engagement.

Rinse And Repeat

Learn from what works, what doesn't and adjust along the way. Repurposing well-performing content across channels. Now you're rolling!

Once you understand the basics, you can fine-tune your method.

There is a lot of overlap between the methods that I will cover in the rest of this chapter - find what works best for you!

Which Content Approach Should You Follow?

Some people have no problem creating well-written, compelling posts, articles, podcasts, or engaging videos for their LinkedIn feed.

But many people struggle with content creation because they're not "publishers" or don't feel comfortable being on video. This is where audio podcasts, webinars and going live can be a great source of content. The fact is people see things all the time, and everybody has opinions, especially regarding issues going on in their industry or niche. I am willing to bet *you* have a few opinions too. This is your opportunity to share!

We'll cover different approaches in this chapter. It's not an either/ or situation. You can create and publish a combination of each.

> **Pro TIP:** Content creation is simply you starting a conversation with your ideal audience. If one approach doesn't work, try another!

Before You Do Anything Else – Know Who Are You Talking To

We already covered a lot when creating your profile about identifying your ideal audience and their pain points. You are now going to use that knowledge in your content creation.

- How are you positioning yourself in the marketplace?
- What do potential clients think about you?
- What is important and relevant to your audience?

The first step to effective positioning and setting yourself apart from the competition is by knowing specifically who your target audience is, which, surprisingly, most people don't really know. They have too wide of a target for fear they will miss out on someone. Just because you manufacture tires, not everyone who owns a car is your target audience. The more specific your niche, the more specialized you become, which means the higher fee you can command.

Niche down to the crucial problems your prospects are facing. Once you are clear on the problems your prospects are dealing with, you are able to align those problems with the solutions you provide.

Now you need a method for conveying that knowledge to educate your buyers to be more informed about the solutions you offer to relieve their problems. But remember, you are NOT selling. You are informing and educating.

That's where insightful content comes into play for B2B marketing. The best type of content is information that bridges the gap between their problem and your solution.

Defining Your "Big Rock" Content Strategy

A content strategy[44] is based on identifying several "buckets" of topics and themes. For instance, I work with a client in the sales training industry. The top three challenges for their clients are PIPELINE, SALES, and PROSPECTING. Those are the three most important topics which happen to align with my client's solutions. Their content strategy is built around those themes.

The company had quite a bit of content previously published. Together, we performed a comprehensive content audit, cataloging all published content along with the engagement metrics for each article, post, video, and podcast on their content inventory tracking sheet.

After categorizing the content information, my client was able to see what they had to work with. This audit helped them see

---

[44]   http://support.syndigate.info/show/
how-to-create-a-documented-content-marketing-strategy

which published content was evergreen (always relevant) and which content needed improvement or updating.

It also helped them see the void as to the type of content topics necessary to align their solution with their prospects' needs.

In this example, the client hosted a successful podcast series. So we used that content as the Big Rock and built a plan around those topics. We also made use of the audience of each of the guests to amplify the reach.

If public speaking is more your thing, then making use of going live with a regular video series (or webinars) might be the way to go. LinkedIn Live is available by request only.[45]

Types Of Content To Share

How do you attract your audience, build credibility and move through your sales funnel today? There are a variety of formats you can use to get your message out there on LinkedIn.

Text – This is pure words, just you sharing your thoughts or advice or discussing your take on industry news. Using emojis is effective in making the post a "Thumb Stopper." Emojis are eye-catching and stop the feed scroller "mid-feed," bringing attention to your post. LinkedIn posts have a 3000-character count limitation[46].

Images – These could be photos, illustrations, infographics, animated GIFs, MEMEs… anything visual. They can be overlaid

---

[45]   https://www.linkedin.com/help/linkedin/answer/100224/
       linkedin-live-video

[46]   https://www.linkedin.com/help/linkedin/answer/100981

with text. Eye-catching images are also Thumb Stoppers to grab the attention of people scrolling through their feed.

Polls[47] – This feature helps you engage with other members by asking them for their perspectives about various topics. Polls help you understand trends and opinions and can be a great conversation starter. They can also be a useful source for creating high value content like articles, visual graphics, and eBooks.

Documents[48] – these are essentially PDFs uploaded as a slideshow. These types of posts stand out in the crowded newsfeed. People tend to stop and take notice, especially if they are thoughtfully produced and visually appealing.

Video – Posting your own videos is very effective at engagement. It could be a "talking head," animation, recording of a webinar, you speaking at an event, etc. The key is to keep it short - 60 seconds or less. Directly uploaded videos tend to perform better than sharing links from Vimeo, YouTube, etc. Also, adding captions is always advised as most videos are viewed with the sound off.

Blog posts – This is long-form content that goes in-depth on an issue and is a great way to establish your thought leadership. Make sure to have a compelling teaser/preview text to encourage people to read the full post. On LinkedIn, this is referred to as an article[49]. You can publish articles from your profile as well as from your Company page.

---

[47] https://www.linkedin.com/help/linkedin/answer/119594
[48] https://www.linkedin.com/help/linkedin/answer/97459
[49] https://www.linkedin.com/help/linkedin/answer/47538

Third-party content – You can share thought-provoking and relevant content from other people, companies, or news organizations. Be certain it is from a reputable source. Earn extra credibility by adding your own commentary. Make sure the content isn't gated behind a paywall.

All these forms of content can be micro or macro content. Sometimes a few sentences will do, and in other cases, you might want to write an entire blog post. The key to determining the best type of content is to ask yourself what serves your audience the best.

It can be challenging to start with a blank canvas. Let's dive into some detailed ideas. I recommend keeping a notebook and pen next to you as we go through these. Or you can write on these pages as I do in my favorite books!

Purposefully Repurpose

That's a tongue twister, but it's an important concept to explain. There is no need to reinvent the wheel when it comes to content creation. When sharing curated content, always provide your own insightful comments demonstrating your expertise, or at the very least, give your audience a reason why they should read what you are sharing - what's in it for them.

To be very clear, when referring to "repurposing," I'm not talking about plagiarizing. This is about using what's out there and presenting it to your audience with your spin on it. It's not simply grabbing an article from an industry publication and sharing the link.

To repurpose successfully, you must add your own insights or add more value in some way. Always attribute the original source material. Listicles and compiled resources are an effective way to leverage third-party sources.

Examples of resourceful curated content I've published for my clients:

- "5 Trends in Home Decor Retail in 2021"
- "6 Questions to Determine if Your CPA is Strategic"
- "7 Best Practices for Generating Non-Dues Revenue for Membership Organizations"
- "Top 20 Supply Chain Industry Podcasts"
- "My top picks for Branding Books"
- "Tradeshow Pros and Cons - from Industry Leaders"

Case Study

Here's an example of how this strategy was implemented for my client who provides technology consulting in the supply chain industry:

While researching for ideas, I noticed the vast number of podcasts specifically for the supply chain/logistics/freight transportation industry. Instead of launching their own podcast, we compiled the 30+ podcasts in a resource list.

Basically, the research entailed going online and finding useful, relevant content that was out there and putting together a comprehensive list, citing all the sources, and publishing it.

We first posted it on their blog[50] (it is now the top source of new traffic on their website!), and then we shared the post on LinkedIn. When sharing it on LinkedIn, I individually called out each of the 30 podcasts in individual comments, tagging the hosts. In turn, the hosts were notified and commented on the post.

That post got thousands of views, hundreds of comments, and even resulted in an inbound quote request for a potential new client! People were asking how they could get on the list. The post was reshared again and again.

That visibility resulted in 3 different podcast hosts reaching out to invite my client as a guest on THEIR podcast. My client didn't have to start their own podcast. Instead, they were able to leverage established audiences by guest appearances on their industry podcasts.

The Top 30 Podcast blog post continues to be the top-visited page on their website. In fact, we just updated the list (it's grown to over 60 podcast shows). We continue to share it as it is evergreen content. The posts consistently generate high visibility and feedback from the audience.

Original Content

Keep two things in mind when creating original content. First, you want to provide insights and educate your audience. Second, you want content that has a high likelihood of being shared and engaged with. Examples of content that accomplish this are:

---

[50] https://jbf-consulting.com/top-30-podcasts-for-supply-chain-logistics-freight-transportation-industry/

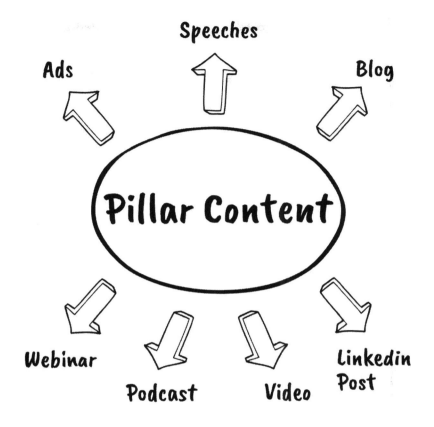

Surveys/Research Reports

This type of content is valuable and likely to be shared.

Case Study

I work with a Top 5 accounting firm client who has carried out surveys and practice management metrics to measure success for their clients. They surveyed their customers about the use of digital tools within their practices. We took the survey results and compiled them into a formal, public-facing comprehensive report. Then we devised a strategy to share the survey results and create content to demonstrate their leadership position in the industry. And now we're using that content and the highlights of that data to engage their target audience by offering them access to the report - the key here is that we are asking permission to see if they have an interest. If they say yes, we then share the link. If they say no, at least we know they check their inbox. But either way, we've earned their credibility.

We can see it's working because we're using LinkedIn's built-in mechanisms to track the consumption of that content. This particular client is subscribed to the Teams Enterprise level of Sales Navigator and has the ability to use SmartLinks[51] for tracking content engagement. We've averaged a 30% conversion rate using this tactic of asking for permission to share high value content.

It's proving to be a very useful tool to generate conversations with their top prospects. So much so that they are already working on the 2022 survey.

Videos

Videos are still a powerful content format for LinkedIn. The nature of a video gives your audience a sense of who you are since they can see you speaking and hear your voice (unless their sound is off).

---

[51] https://www.linkedin.com/help/sales-navigator/answer/a130001/smart-links-insights

Case Study

My client is an executive recruiter who works in a specific geographic market. He specializes in placing C-suite technology leaders who ideally continue to work with him to build out their teams. He values developing relationships with his clients and prospects, so we formulated a strategy of conveying leadership concepts and some of the pain points his audience is concerned with when recruiting top talent and building strong teams.

At first, we published articles, but it wasn't resonating with his audience. We refined the strategy by using short (less than 60-second) videos which are shared on his social platforms where his audience consumes content. He uses old-school index cards to plan, organize, and script his videos. This helps keep them short and focused.

He records them in batches on his smartphone using a teleprompter app. We then transcribe them, add subtitle captions, and post them directly to LinkedIn using a branded hashtag to catalog the video collection. We also created a YouTube channel so his followers can access the complete library of content.

When we started working together, he was awkward on camera. Yet, he was willing to put himself out there, get out of his comfort zone, and commit to creating content. Over the two years we've been working together, he's become more confident; he's progressed over time. With each video, he refined his delivery and timing.

And the best part is he has established himself as a thought leader amongst his key economic buyers. Now when he's out and about in his community, people recognize him from his videos. And this visibility, credibility, and trustworthiness have led to new business opportunities.

To take it a step further, we are self-publishing a book compilation organized by themes of the edited transcripts. This book will be used as a value-add "gift" to his current clients and as a conversation starter with high-level prospects.

This is an example of finding the type of content the audience will engage with and trying a unique medium such as video. His perceived competition was not doing anything like this.

In-depth Article

Case Study

My client runs a sales agency specializing in the creative arts in the retail space. Take note of how specific their target niche is. To help them become visible experts and generate a whole series of content pieces, we tapped into industry data about the viability of trade shows. Mind you, this was pre-COVID when in-person trade shows were still a thing.

We identified a batch of his connections and asked them about the pros and cons of attending and exhibiting at trade shows through direct messaging on LinkedIn. The response to our message campaign was off the charts. Not only did people reply, but some provided valuable soundbites.

We turned the message responses into a comprehensive long-form article. We sourced industry data, trends, quotes from industry leaders, and added infographics.

The content strategy was to explore the challenges and pain points that my client's prospects were dealing with and that as a result of reading this article, we wanted them to find the information beneficial.

We published a comprehensive article on LinkedIn since they didn't have a blog. And then, we sent direct messages to all the participants in the initial outreach offering to share the article. A lot of conversations started. Great, timely content. This didn't happen by accident.

Taking it a step further, we created a variety of shareable snippets, featured quotes from respondents, and used that as content on LinkedIn as well, with their permission, of course.

We made an effort to strategically connect my client with the appropriate targets – trade show vendors in manufacturing and retail – to find something important to them. And it was because this is how they did business.

When we got their feedback, we followed up and delivered what we said we would do by creating this content, which led to two new five-figure contracts for my client.

And throughout 2020 and into this year, with trade shows canceled, we pivoted the strategy to ask the audience their opinion on the effectiveness of virtual events. What did they see as the pros and cons? We even produced a guide to share with them outlining how to make the most of virtual events.

Webinars

Don't have time to do your own webinars? Remember that you can curate instead and give key take-aways of other relevant webinars or a list of valuable webinars your audience can attend.

Case Study

A client who provides publication project management to the Chamber of Commerce industry tapped into the main pain point, namely, "how to generate non-dues revenue." Together we launched a video podcast series, the client interviewing various chamber executives about their success with generating non-dues revenue. Such interviews have afforded him the opportunity to converse with high-value prospects while building a sizable body of valuable content.

After recording the episodes, we share the videos on YouTube and upload the audio track to a podcast-sharing platform. We also transcribe the video and convert it to show notes and a long-form article. And we promote the podcast by sharing highlights on social media platforms and in monthly email campaigns.

The visibility has been tremendous, and it's elevated his exposure amongst his prospective clients.

Success Stories

When a prospect can see themselves in your success story, you have a higher chance of getting them interested in a conversation with you. Use success stories strategically. They should avoid a specific company name. The ultimate goal is to help the reader see how your solution and services can be applied to their needs.

There are various options to feature case studies or success stories in your content, such as:

- Spotlight your referral relationships
- Showcase a new partnership
- Highlight a new hire and what they bring to the team
- Share your trusted resources and tools

Not only can this type of content build new relationships, but it can also strengthen the existing relationships you have.

Once you create the content, share it with the person/organization/business that you feature. They may choose to share on their content channels as well, boosting your results. They may also comment on your original post, which will add to your credibility.

Books You Are Reading

Do you stay up to date in your field by reading new books in your niche? Studies show that many professionals do – and those who don't probably know they should. You can serve as a guide to the themes in those books.

You can provide such guidance by writing reviews, critiques, or summaries. They all provide an opportunity to show your expertise while delivering value to your audience.

If you like the book you read, share your content with the author when you finish. You never know what kind of connections you may form.

Trends In Your Industry

Does your industry change often? Are there trigger events throughout the year? What about important aspects that might not be general knowledge for your clients yet?

Your content is a great opportunity to share your thoughts, ideas, predictions, and evaluation of the trends you see.

FAQs

Every industry has those questions that keep coming up over and over again. The good news for you is that this is an area ripe for content creation. Some things to use as mental prompts include:

- Discussing client concerns – what keeps them up at night – turn it into a positive post
- Responses to questions often asked before beginning to work with you
- Explaining a popular acronym, jargon, credential, or visual diagram in your field
- Listing pre-client prep tasks or client checklists for clients and potential clients.

Pro TIP: Keep a file of questions you can add to whenever you get an email, phone call, or in-person question from a client. Make sure to get your team in on the fun too!

Getting To Know You

Content can also be a way to get to know you as a professional or your company as a whole. This can make you more approachable and allow your potential clients the feeling that they already know you. When you have someone's trust, you are more than halfway to closing the deal. Some examples are:

- A behind the scenes look at a "day-in-the-life" of your work, your office, your team
- Your thought process or meaning behind your logo or business name
- Discussions about any core values, philosophy, or a sense of mission that drives your business

You may be surprised how much these types of posts will resonate with your audience.

Refreshing Evergreen Content

There is another method to repurposing content - revive your evergreen content.

To my knowledge, Rebecca Lieb, was the first to equate the Thanksgiving feast[52] to the process of creating Big Rock content. "I use a Thanksgiving analogy," she said. "You cook up this giant bird to serve up on one glorious occasion and then proceed to slice and dice this thing for weeks on end. If you are like most families you are going to be repurposing this bird as leftovers for quite some time, creating everything from sandwiches, to soups, and more.

---

[52] https://business.linkedin.com/marketing-solutions/blog/l/leftover-turkey-a-content-marketers-dream

Your content marketing strategy can be thought of in the same way." Once you inventory everything published, see what is relevant and useful to your target audience and determine how to repurpose it. Sometimes "old" material simply needs to be refreshed – what I refer to as "evergreen" content.

Carving Up Your Content

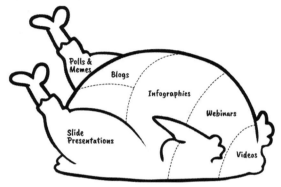

Similarly, take existing content and "carve out" blog posts, infographics, webinars, videos, pull quotes, checklists, worksheets, quizzes, presentation decks, etc. that you can share on your digital platforms.

The easy way to do this is to start with a video recording that aligns with the problems and challenges your target niche faces. The purpose of the content is to establish that you understand your audience's pain points with your unique point of view. You are the subject matter expert.

As discussed earlier, evergreen content is content that stands the test of time. Certain things, at their core, remain relevant long term.

> **Pro TIP:** Create an expiration date. Keep a spreadsheet of all your evergreen content and include an "expiration date" if needed - for example, a post about 2020 statistics will need to be updated on Jan. 1, 2022.

Extend The Life Of Your Content

There are many ways to take content with a great foundation and give it a proverbial fresh coat of paint.

Here are just a few ideas to get you started:

- Update old articles with new information
- Transcribe past video content to text format and publish
- Convert your old blog posts into guides or e-books
- Turn your written content into videos and podcasts
- Use your internal data to create case studies
- Collect your interviews and notes to create an "expert advice" eBook
- Transform a Quora Q&A into a blog post
- Dust off slide decks and convert to PDF documents
- Turn a slideshow into an infographic
- Build an infographic or checklist from a blog post
- Turn your text content into animated text videos
- Conduct podcast interviews with people you have written text info about in the past
- Pull out quotes from longer-form content to turn into micro-content
- Break up long articles into shorter posts and infographics
- Transform your webinars into valuable video training series
- Republish your blog posts as LinkedIn articles

There's always a way to take your original content and present it in a fresh new format. Leverage the hard work you put into the first piece you published. After all, you don't need to reinvent the wheel every time!

In each case, you take one of something and turn it into many – or many of something and turn it into one.

Let's look at a couple of examples.

In this example, you start with a webinar or other recorded presentation that you have done in the past. And then you start transforming it into various types of new content.

- Start with a video (a webinar or recorded presentation)
- Live stream the webinar
- Publish the slides on LinkedIn as a document
- Turn your slides into social media graphics
- Upload the full video on YouTube or Vimeo
- Embed the video on your website
- Share short video clips on social media
- Separate the audio from the video to use as a podcast
- Transcribe the video/audio recording
- Publish the transcript as a blog post
- Break the content down into multiple blog posts
- Create an infographic of pull quotes or bullet point lists
- Share the information as an email drip campaign series
- Create branded graphics, quotes, images, and charts to share on social media

You now have taken one foundational part of core content and turned it into many pieces of content.

Content In Reverse - From Many To One

Sometimes shorter content can serve as fabric panels to weave a longer piece of content together. This not only helps your ideal audience make connections between concepts and ideas but sets you apart as a thought leader.

Here are some examples of ways to do this:

- Combine a series of related blog posts into an eBook
- Present a library of interviews into a digital summit
- Collect a group of social media images into a slideshow
- Feature a series of inspirational quotes as a tip guide or eBook
- Convert an email series into a PDF guide and use it as a lead magnet
- Compile a group of customer/audience questions into a guide or blog post
- Transform a graphic into a checklist or worksheet

The examples above can turn any of these into an epic campaign. The keyword is *campaign*. If you are taking the time to put these longer form types of content together, make sure that your calls to action are ready to maximize your ROI.

Benefits Of High-Quality Content

Does this all seem like a lot of time?

It can be, but creating relevant, high-quality content has many benefits:

- Relevant expertise is a deciding factor for a client to hire you. Expertise is one of those invisible qualities. Through purposeful content, you can demonstrate your mastery as a thought leader.

- Compelling content drives new prospects and referrals. When you produce educational content, it helps your audience gain a deeper understanding.
- Content increases your visibility. As more people come into your network and engage with your content, they'll ultimately discover that you might be able to help them.
- Premium content opens higher quality opportunities. Once a prospect has engaged with your content, they become better educated about what you do and how you think.
- Quality content educates and informs your readers by sharing something important to them they weren't aware of (that they aren't getting from another source).

By publishing this type of content, you're elevating your authority positioning in the minds of your prospects. The person who publishes is the authority, and you – and your LinkedIn profile – become visible.

When you **Elevate** your profile through content, you can then **Expand** your network. Expanding happens because your content is shared and commented on, which in turn extends your reach and exposes you to new people who may happen to have an interest in your services.

When someone interacts with your content, it's almost like an endorsement or passive referral.

Pro TIP: Always be sure to acknowledge people for shares and respond to comments to keep building that positive rapport.

Then **Engage** your audience by further sharing that content on the platform. Use it in your messaging, letting people know you've published new content with interesting topics. See how it all plays together?

It's a talking point when you connect with people on LinkedIn. And, because you address pain points they may be experiencing, those people are more likely to engage with you and participate in a conversation.

At the very core of the Triple-E Method™ is, of course, compelling content.

Content, created strategically, provides context for conversations. It's one of the most effective ways to start the right kind of conversations with your target audience, including prospects and potential referral partners, at the right time.

Original content is always stronger in this regard. When you are the content creator, the expert behind the ideas, people will interact with you differently and think of you more as a subject matter expert.

Over time you will grow your followers and receive inbound invites to connect from your target audience. That's how I've built my LinkedIn network to more than 35,000 followers.

If you find what you're doing isn't getting the results you desire, step back and examine these key areas of your three-legged stool:

- Assess your profile. Is it resonating with your audience in a way that is meaningful to them?

- Review your connection database. Are you connecting with the right decision-makers in your target market?
- Audit your content engagement. Is your messaging getting a response? Is the content you share aligned with your audience's pain points?

You cannot improve what you don't assess. Once you examine these key areas, take that knowledge and use it to reverse engineer your actions and make necessary adjustments.

When you are one of the few in your niche making a consistent effort and giving more than you take, so to speak – you stand out. A cadence of outreach and engagement on a regular basis will not only help you gain ground with your prospects but will also train the LinkedIn algorithm.[53] [54]

This consistent activity will reward you by distributing your content in the newsfeed to a broader audience beyond your 1st-degree network.

Consistent activity is what keeps you showing up in the feed of your network. Sharing insights and your industry knowledge is what makes you credible. Engaging with your audience builds trust. Trust leads to business opportunities.

When your prospect can no longer stand their problem and solving it becomes a priority for them, you will be top of mind. Then your prospect will remember you and come to you for help. But only if you are committed to being consistent and relevant.

---

[53] https://www.linkedin.com/pulse/
linkedin-algorithm-explained-how-make-work-you-courtney-johnson/
[54] https://www.brandwatch.com/blog/linkedin-algorithm/

Anybody can set themselves apart in this way, and it yields results if you work at it.

How You Stand Out From The Noise

You may have heard of Imposter Syndrome, where even experts in a field seriously doubt their ability despite a mountain of evidence to the contrary. Who *doesn't* feel like they have Imposter Syndrome? I admit I have experienced it. It's real, but it's not.

It's a fear of how people will perceive you. It's a fear that maybe you'll make a mistake… or appear foolish. Or that you are a fake. It's common. It's the conversation you have with yourself in your head and far from reality. Just recognize it, own it, and push past it.

So how do you stand out above the noise?

How can you differentiate yourself from your competitors on LinkedIn? Not only that, but how do you demonstrate the depth of industry knowledge and your unique expertise? And how do you become the go-to provider in your area of specialty?

Now that your profile is ready for prime time, you can dip your toe in the water. Familiarize yourself with your homepage feed. What type of content are you seeing? Notice who is posting content and look at the engagement (comments and reactions) of the posts.

My guess is that if you managed to build a business, you have found ways to connect with others. Now you simply have to put those same skills to work on LinkedIn.

Not all content is created equal. It's all about creating what nobody else is doing, whether that's a video, compiling resources, polling your audience, publishing an insightful article, useful industry report, eBook, whitepaper, or resource guide. Create the type of content that will position you as a helpful, go-to expert resource.

Always start with a coherent strategy that aligns with your overall business goals, and then build from there. Creating content without a strategy will not be effective in helping you become a visible expert.

Become that trusted resource an editor would seek a quote from when covering an issue in your industry, or a podcast host would want to invite you as a guest on their show.

Most people are afraid of putting content out there because they either want it to be perfect or are worried they will say something someone disagrees with. If that's what's holding you back, I encourage you to overcome that fear. The delete and edit buttons are powerful tools!

Measuring The Results Of Your Content

At the end of the day, you are probably asking - where's the ROI? I am investing time and possibly money into developing great content. How do I know whether or not it is working?

You want to know who's looking at your content and engaging with it. Identifying key performance indicators (KPIs) is how you track your activity to measure improvement. LinkedIn provides basic metrics such as views, reactions, and comments.

Over time, you'll start to see business growth accelerating – the ultimate benchmark.

We will cover KPIs on LinkedIn in more depth later in this book.

Test, improve, test, improve, and test more. Do more of what's working. Do less of what's not.

Do I *Really* Need Content?

Some people hesitate to take this on. And honestly, sometimes this is an area where it is worth it to hire an experienced content creator to handle.

Where to start? What to say? You can come up with a million excuses. I've heard them all. But by doing nothing, how do you expect to start showing up in the newsfeed? If you aren't actively engaged, how will you showcase your uniqueness and authenticity?

Consider this – in 2019, LinkedIn sessions increased 25 percent year-over-year, with 358 billion feed updates viewed. But only 3 million users (out of the 774+ million) share content every week. This means that only about 1% of LinkedIn's 260 million monthly users share posts and those 3 million or so users net 9 billion impressions.[55] That's a lot of eyeballs for a small active group.

Get in the game while organic reach is still possible.

---

[55]   https://kinsta.com/blog/linkedin-statistics/

Of course, as with many things in life, simply showing up is the first step. But standing out in a memorable way is what sets you apart. Don't be that person who stands in the corner of the room, watching but not participating.

By consistently being active in posting, commenting, educating, and giving of your knowledge... the more places you show up... the more you increase visibility... the more you are top of mind. When your prospect has a problem they think you can solve based on what you've been sharing, you want to be the one they will contact.

Action Items:

- ☐ Commit to content creation
- ☐ Determine what your audience needs to hear
- ☐ Choose a strategy that works for you
- ☐ Catalog the content you already have
- ☐ Decide what new content you want to produce
- ☐ Transform your content from one to many and many to one to multiply your content
- ☐ Allocate necessary resources (time, expertise, money) for content creation
- ☐ Measure your results

PART TWO

EXPAND

First impressions matter. That is why **Elevating** your profile and presence on LinkedIn is the first step. But first impressions will only take you so far. You will need to do the work of expanding your network.

Without being connected to a network, your profile is a bunch of code on a website. It is the relationships with people that make business happen. **Expanding** your network goes hand-in-hand with **Engaging** with them, which we cover in the next section. In the meantime, let's go over why it even matters.

Aside from its primary business focus, LinkedIn is a unique social network. When used strategically, it's the ideal platform to promote your personal brand and company amongst other business professionals, rainmakers, and industry leaders. It's even helpful in recruiting top talent.

Fear Can Render You Powerless

I used to teach scrapbooking, and while children would just plunge ahead and not worry about "messing up," I found adults to be the hardest to teach. They wanted everything just right. As a result, they were paralyzed with fear of making a mistake and found it difficult to move forward on their craft projects, worried they weren't doing it "right."

I think fear of failure is why so many people are reluctant to put themselves out on LinkedIn.

I get it. You're not sure what to say or do on LinkedIn. Yet, you want to establish your authority in your niche – and sometimes that means challenging the status quo, stirring things up to get a conversation going – but you're nervous about saying the "wrong thing" when you do so.

You freeze trying to know what to post, say to your connections, respond to comments, or comment effectively on the posts of others. You're scared of appearing foolish in such a public forum. It's the intimidation we all face when trying something new and outside our comfort zone. The critic is in our head!

Three points here.

1. It's not so scary. You're overthinking this. Just be yourself.
2. You don't have to come up with "original" content to get results.
3. If you "mess up," it can be fixed by editing or deleting.

In this section, we will do a deep dive into **Expanding** your network. This is where all the hard work on your profile and content starts to pay off. Here's what we'll cover:

Nurturing Your Most Valuable Connections

In this chapter, we will go over the importance of focusing your network, determining the best contacts to build relationships with, and how to connect with people based on what matters most to them.

Grow Your Business Through Building Your Network

You probably have a stronger existing network than you realize – are you leaving money on the table? While I always work to show that relationships matter most, this is LinkedIn, not Facebook. At the end of the day, the reason you are here is to grow your business by providing value. Now you can learn how to re-engage these connections.

Activating New Connections

There is a saying that if you are not growing, you are dying. In this chapter, we explore how to use tools both inside and outside LinkedIn to continue to meet new potential clients, referral resources, and partners.

Nurturing Your Most Valuable Connections

You have probably heard of the 80/20 rule – that 80% of your success comes from 20% of your effort. This can be true with your business connections as well. In order to make the best ROI of your effort on LinkedIn, it is important to know who we are trying to reach and why.

Finding Your Ideal Customers On Linkedin

To find your ideal customers, you need to know who they are. Defining buyer personas is the starting point for a successful LinkedIn campaign. If you're not familiar with the term persona, think of it as a fictional character based on your ideal target prospect. A clear understanding of your target audience is fundamental to finding and building a quality network.

By understanding your target prospect's expectations, concerns, and motivations, you are essentially building a comprehensive profile of your target customer.

Knowing who your persona is can be helpful for both finding them on LinkedIn as well as crafting laser-focused messaging and content specifically relevant to this one person. With 774+ million members on LinkedIn, it's a crowded space. Without a persona, you're going in with a blindfold.

Step 1: Know Your Current Customer

To create a persona, start with research to collect information about your current customers to give you a way to identify prospective customers. You might accomplish this through client surveys, reviewing past records and invoices, or interviewing clients about why they work with you.

If you have a team, involve them in this process.

When you are a new business, you might not have as many past clients to review. In that case, choose a competitor and profile their customers. Look at online reviews of their business and see who sings their praises. Also, look at the negative reviews, as these will give you ideas how to differentiate your client base.

Step 2: Use LinkedIn Tools to Refine Your Strategy

Use filters, exclusions and Boolean search strings to find people on LinkedIn, particularly in the Sales Navigator edition. This is where investing in the premium subscription of Sales Navigator can come in handy. Sales Navigator has filters for inclusion and exclusion. There's also an ability to create specific lists and cross-search based on other criteria. This allows you to pinpoint them down to the finest detail.

When refining your strategy, we will start with your network but revisit this strategy to expand it.

> **Pro TIP:** If you subscribe to Sales Navigator[56] and decide to cancel that subscription, all the data will be lost, including any inbox messages generated on Sales Navigator.

Step 3: Determine Which Customers/Clients are Your Ideal Target Focus

Many people are concerned that they won't be able to find customers if they narrow their focus. Yet if you don't, then you will not have a focused network.

Not every type of prospect is necessarily a target on LinkedIn. Certain industries perform better than others. For instance, let's say your target decision-maker is a Food Safety role at multi-unit restaurants. A quick search shows that although there are profiles that meet those criteria, they are not active. That would be a hard nut to crack and probably not a viable reach on LinkedIn.

No Pain No Gain

Once you know who you want to reach on LinkedIn, you'll want to be clear about what problem they are experiencing that your service or product will solve. Is there anything preventing them from achieving success in what they want to accomplish?

When that pain point becomes a "bleeding neck" that the prospect can no longer tolerate, that is when they will be receptive to finding a solution, ideally YOU!

Not all prospects are aware that they may have such a problem, or the problem may not be happening at the exact moment you

---

[56] https://www.linkedin.com/business/sales/blog/sales-navigator/introducing-a-brief-history-of-linkedin-sales-navigator-infogra

make the connection. Many prospect pain points are similar. However, there's no one-size-fits-all solution to solving your customers' pain. The good news is that you know your customers better than anyone, so do your research and start helping them accomplish what they really want to do.

> **Pro TIP:** Take the time to ask questions that help uncover the root cause rather than jumping too quickly to a solution.

Pain points identify challenges. Now that you know that you'll want to dig a little deeper and find out the goals your customers are trying to achieve and what obstacles are preventing them from doing so.

Knowing your customers' goals and obstacles will help you to better understand how you can help relieve their pain. Do you have the resources and skills to help your customers overcome their pain points? How can you help your customers achieve their goals?

This is where providing pain point insights and informative, educational content will help your prospects realize they may have a problem that needs fixing. You will build credibility by imparting your knowledge of their specific issues and introducing them to similar challenges you have solved for other clients like them.

It's very important to understand that the insights you share are not in any way a sales pitch. That's a turn-off, especially if they haven't sought you out. Your solution should help relieve their pain. You want to find the gap between your prospect's problems that you can solve and your solution.

Let's examine possible pain points here in greater detail. These pain points are a starting point to get you thinking in the right frame of mind, from the prospect's point of view. Each situation is unique, yet experience shows that many prospects' problems are complex layers best viewed holistically. You may find many of your prospects are experiencing similar problems. However, the root causes can vary.

Pain points tend to fall into one of these buckets:

Process - your prospect may have processes that impact other areas of their business, causing more problems. For instance, there may be several decision makers, or they may have numerous processes of reviewing proposals, or they may require board approval.

Productivity - your prospects may be using a solutions provider that is not performing up to expectation. This pain is causing your prospect to lose out on opportunities or drain resources and revenue.

Financial - perhaps your prospect is not operating at their highest potential and leaking profits or wasting money on services that are not producing a decent return.

Support - your prospect may not be getting the support they need from their current supplier. Things are falling through the cracks, or there is a lack of accountability. This may be a costly problem as well.

Start thinking about how you might position your services as a solution to your prospects' problems and what is needed to give them peace of mind.

Understanding Audiences On Linkedin

If you're looking for your B2B audience on social media, LinkedIn is the right place to find them because its database is a goldmine of opportunities.

LinkedIn's high-quality data lets you target professional audiences with the most precision. This precision is better than any other platform[57] because it's the only online platform where nearly 61 million users are Senior Level influencers[58] and 40 million hold decision-making profiles.

There is some filtering you can perform on the free version of LinkedIn, but you will encounter limitations quickly, and the results will not be as good as when using the premium Sales Navigator. Navigator's filters[59] of inclusions, exclusions, and Boolean strings give you access to rich demographic data and filter by job function, seniority, years of experience, geographic location down to the zip code, industry, and company name.

You can target members in many ways:

- by the LinkedIn groups they belong to
- their field of study and alumni
- the skills they self-identify with

---

[57] https://business.linkedin.com/marketing-solutions/audience
[58] https://foundationinc.co/lab/b2b-marketing-linkedin-stats/
[59] https://www.linkedin.com/help/linkedin/answer/75814/

- years of experience
- zip code or region

You can also match your target list against the 13M+ company pages to achieve Account-Based[60] marketing goals.

Think Quality NOT Quantity When Building Your Network

To get results — more conversations with your target audience — you need to build a strategic network on LinkedIn carefully. A network that focuses on quality, not quantity. Sure, it takes work on the front end, but the quality of your network impacts who you can connect with, and to some degree, what shows up in your newsfeed.

Building a network starts with knowing your target market, as we just covered it with audience personas. You can have multiple target markets in the niches you work in based on industry, geographic area, job title, employee count, or whatever criteria you want to use.

Here are some typical issues I've seen when initially working with my clients:

- They haven't built their network strategically. They have connections that are not in their geographic market or are in unrelated industries. Starting with a disconnected foundation makes it hard to grow an effective network. It's not impossible. It's just more challenging.

---

[60] https://business.linkedin.com/marketing-solutions/ad-targeting/account-targeting

- They have a very small network of unrelated connections (not real prospects). This limits growth potential. Having a proximity or common connection to invite, preferably 2nd-degree, will yield better outreach results.
- They have a sizable network of 1st-degree connections but haven't engaged with most of them in a long time, if at all. There are many lost opportunities from not reactivating conversations with this low-hanging fruit.

If you're just starting, try to build your network with people you know, such as past clients, colleagues, alumni, or people you've worked with, as well as joining Groups where your target audience belongs. This will open your 2nd-degree proximity.

Once you reach the first milestone of 500+ connections, start becoming more selective about who you connect with. When someone sends you an invitation to connect, as flattering as that might be, make sure it aligns with your overall LinkedIn strategy.

- Look at their profile
- Look at their activity feed
- If it makes sense to connect, accept their invitation
- If not, click 'ignore' to remove the invitation
- If they respond with a sales pitch, immediately disconnect and unfollow
- Report them if their content is offensive

The Power Of Your Network

You may be familiar with the term "six degrees of separation."[61] On LinkedIn, people in your network are called connections.

---

[61]   https://en.wikipedia.org/wiki/Six_degrees_of_separation

Your network consists of your 1st-degree, 2nd-degree, and 3rd-degree connections, as well as fellow members of your LinkedIn groups.

Each degree of connection in your network, including who you can communicate with, is based on their proximity in your network. You'll see an icon next to each person's name denoting the degree on their profile and in search results.

1st-degree connections are actual connections of yours. 2nd-degree are not your connections. Instead, they are connected to someone you're directly connected to. 3rd-degree are people on LinkedIn who only have connections in your 2nd-degree network.[62]

When a user accepts an invitation from another user, this establishes a first-level connection; the user is indirectly connected to the other user's connections with what LinkedIn terms second-level and third-level connections.

Fellow members of your LinkedIn Groups are considered part of your network because you're members of the same Group. The Highlights section of a member profile may display the Groups you're both a part of. You can communicate with mutual Group members directly by sending a message directly through the Group. Right now, this is the only benefit of joining Groups. Choose Groups to join where your ideal target audience is.

LinkedIn Member (Out of Network) - This means you have no proximity to these LinkedIn members who fall outside the

---

[62]   https://en.wikipedia.org/wiki/LinkedIn

categories listed above. Profiles out of your network have limited visibility but you can invite them to join your network if they have an 'open' profile. If the option is available, you can also send them an InMail to introduce yourself.

Now that you know how the network works, you'll need a strategy for building your network. On average, every new connection you make expands your network by 150 connections +/- 2nd and 3rd-degree. This is why it is critical to have a networking growth strategy.

As your connections increase, your personal network explodes

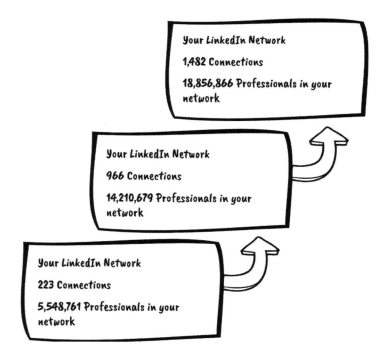

Source: www.theconversioncompany.com

Action Items:

- ☐ Analyze your current customers to build customer profiles
- ☐ Determine your target audience
- ☐ Create your target audience persona(s)
- ☐ Understand their key pain points
- ☐ Know how your solutions align with those pain points
- ☐ Define your network growth strategy

Growing Your Business By Building Your Network

Now that you know who you are trying to reach and how you can help them, it is time to start developing your network. There are a variety of tools within LinkedIn that make this easier.

Using LinkedIn Suggestions

LinkedIn automatically suggests people you may want to connect with using patterns from your activity and network. I rarely find these recommendations to be helpful. But if you are curious, check out their profiles, and if you find they fit your target, send an invitation. Always personalize the invite and explain why you want to connect.

How To Expand Your Network

Curating a high-quality network can be achieved if you think creatively. Here are four ways.

1. Find content with high engagement and relevant to your audience. Look at who engaged (reactions and comments). Direct message those who fit your target audience and mention something from the post to start a conversation. Or, if you're not connected, comment on the post. This will trigger a notification to all who have engaged. Wait a day for it to circulate in the feed, and

then reference the post as you personalize your outreach to them.

2. Identify people whose audience is similar to yours. If their connections are set to "open" visibility, you can perform a filtered search of 2nd-degree connections of your connections.[63] If you know your connection well enough, you can reach out to them to see if they would be open to making an introduction on your behalf or get permission to mention their name and directly outreach yourself.

3. Find LinkedIn Groups where your target audience belongs. If you are a member of the same Group, you can send a direct message to other members. Don't be spammy. Always put yourself on the receiving end of how your outreach will be perceived.

4. One of the most effective ways to connect with a prospect is to look at their activity feed and, if they are active, comment on their posts. This will trigger a notification that you've viewed their profile and engaged with their content. However, if they are not actively sharing content, then look closely at their profile. Read their recommendations if they have any and find a common thread of interest or curiosity to mention in your invite.

> **Pro TIP:** Make sure your visibility settings are set to full view. Otherwise, your view of their profile will show up as "anonymous."

---

[63] https://www.linkedin.com/help/linkedin/answer/4820/view-your-connection-s-connections

Outta Sight Outta Mind

People and companies (if multiple decision-makers are involved) take time to make decisions - your challenge is to remain top of mind without being annoying. Instead, be informative and resourceful.

B2B buyers progress more than 70% of the way through the decision-making process before ever engaging with your company.[64]

Here is the key data point to pay attention to - most of this due diligence research is done online and on social platforms. According to Google, 90% of B2B online researchers use search specifically to research business purchases.[65] Remember what you learned about Company pages earlier. This is why your presence on LinkedIn is so important.

And 56% of professionals[66] said a business executive's presence on social media positively influences their purchase decision, and 66% of professionals[67] said they would be more likely to recommend a company or brand if they followed a company executive on social media.

This is why you must grow your network while also consistently publishing and sharing insights relevant to your market niche

---

[64]   https://blog.passle.net/post/102fqjl/
b2b-buyers-do-70-of-their-research-online

[65]   https://www.omnicoreagency.com/linkedin-statistics/

[66]   https://business.linkedin.com/marketing-solutions/cx/21/03/
executive-thought-leadership-quick-start-guide

[67]   https://business.linkedin.com/content/dam/me/business/en-us/
marketing-solutions/cx/2021/images/namer-pdfs/executive-thought-
leadership-quick-start-guide.pdf

to ensure you remain top of mind. I cannot stress this enough. Remaining top of mind and network building through content publication and comments is the essence of what makes LinkedIn so valuable.

My most successful clients understand that it's a long game, not a quick fix. LinkedIn is just one part of the business development equation, and it's often not a linear journey for the buyer. You want to activate as many multiple touchpoints as possible.

Get into the habit of a methodical and strategic approach to using LinkedIn. With this habit, you stay in communication and on the radar of your high-value prospects so that when your solution becomes a priority for the B2B buyer, you will get the call.

People want to work with those who have the authority – experts in their niche - leaders in the industry. Is that going to be you? You better believe it is.

Withdrawing Aged Invites

Old invites are like dirty laundry - they don't get better with age. If someone hasn't accepted your invite to connect within three weeks of sending it, you should withdraw your invitation. This will keep your sent invites list manageable and allow for sending another invite later. Likewise, you should process your inbound invites regularly.

Join Groups To Expand Your Network

Wait, What? I thought LinkedIn Groups were dead? Well, sort of. LinkedIn Groups are no longer the forums they once were years ago after they became spam fests.

So why would joining Groups be something beneficial?

For one thing, if you are a member of a Group, you can invite that person to connect. Connecting from a Group is particularly useful if you are starting with a small network and have limited second-degree connections. Another benefit is that you can message other group members directly for free.

The strategy for joining a Group is finding the Groups where your ideal audience and prospects are members. The right Groups give you proximity and visibility.

Should You Remove Connections?

We are talking about growing our network - so the more, the better, right?

When I worked at the Austin Chamber of Commerce as the VP of Communications, I connected with every company and business member. During the three years I worked there, I added over 1,500 connections. That strategy made sense for where I was at that time.

Did I remove those people when I moved to New York? No. Why not?

Remember the 2nd-degree proximity? If I removed a connection, I would lose that proximity, which would hinder my ability to grow my network. It also turns out several of my connections moved away to cities outside of Texas, and a few even moved to NYC. So unless you have just cause for removing someone, just leave them in your network. You never know where or to whom it might lead.

If you don't want their activity showing up in your newsfeed, simply UNFOLLOW them instead of removing them. You maintain the connection and your feed is streamlined.

I always refer to this basic philosophy:

- What is your purpose?
- What are your business goals?
- Why are you on LinkedIn in the first place?

Use your strategy as you identify and grow your network. From there, you can determine what type of person you want to connect with.

Do You Have More Potential Connections Than You Think?

Often, you don't realize that your potential connections could be outside your usual marketing niche. For example, I have a client targeting engineering firms in a specific part of the country. He provided expertise with CAD drawings. And that gave me an idea.

He could also try to connect with construction firms, architects, and even people in commercial real estate because those people have similar needs and networks. They will likely be connected with engineers they work with or know.

Taking that idea a step further, we looked at industry associations with LinkedIn Groups. We also made a list of speakers and influencers at industry events.

I had a client recently who put this to work. He downloaded his database and started by sorting by title and company. Then he started sending direct messages to start conversations with those he hadn't talked to in a while. During this outreach, he talked to a former colleague. That individual had moved on to a new company as well, and they found some great synergy. My client was able to land a new project based on the existing relationship – and none of it would have happened if he hadn't taken the first step to reach out.

Action Items:

- ☐ Find relevant content that has high engagement
- ☐ Use content engagement to get the attention of your prospect
- ☐ Join LinkedIn Groups where your target audience belongs
- ☐ Ask for introductions to connections from your network
- ☐ Clear out aged invites after three weeks
- ☐ Re-engage with contacts that you have lost touch with

Activating New Connections

Using LinkedIn to connect with your existing and 2nd-degree connections is a good place to start. Now it is time to start building beyond that.

Human To Human

Above all, remember that there is a real person on the receiving end of your messages. The more relevant and specific your message is to the recipient, the better chance you have of them accepting your connection request. Your profile will also be a factor.

If the person on the other end senses you want to "sell" them something, your request will most likely be ignored. If your invites are flagged as "I don't know this person" too often, you may risk LinkedIn limiting your ability to send invites by requiring an email for each prospect.

For benchmark purposes, an average connection rate is 30% - which varies by industry and other mitigating factors. So that means out of every 100 invitations you send, about 30 will become connections. And out of the 30% who accept your invitation, you can expect a 2%-10% engagement rate if you use the right strategy. Many variables impact this, so these figures are just for benchmarking.

Taking the time to craft personalized messages when you reach out to connect with someone will increase the likelihood of conversion. Customize your invitation based on what you see on their profile, what they've posted, or whatever your reason is for wanting to connect with them.

Your message should read like you are talking to a real person one-to-one, not like a script going out to the masses. Keep it simple, as if you've texted it from your mobile device. Keep the "ask" to one main goal - to get the connection request accepted.

LinkedIn Is Not Facebook

LinkedIn is a virtual network for professionals. It's more like attending a business networking event full of high-powered executives. You should be on your best behavior as if what you say and do could be shown on the jumbotron in Times Square.

LinkedIn is not Facebook. It's not a casual backyard barbecue where you might use colorful language, wear shorts, flip flops, and share gossip or private information.

If you behave this way on LinkedIn, you can expect the same results as if you did it in a business network meeting.

When you reach out to connect with people on LinkedIn, you need some context, a reason why you're contacting them, and what drew you to them. Take the extra effort to find out a bit about them. You'd be surprised at how many people don't look at profiles before sending invites. By personalizing your invitation to connect, you've increased your odds of making the connection.

Pro TIP: After making a new connection, acknowledge them as you would if you met someone at a professional event - you would extend your hand to greet them. Don't jump in with a sales pitch.

Personalizing your invites and keeping interactions professional goes back to cultivating relationships, knowing your objective, and getting prospects to engage with you. All relationships are unique to the individuals involved. They start with possibilities, strengthen over time with familiarity, and become credible and ultimately build trust.

> As Bob Burg says, "All things being equal, people do business with, and refer business to people they know, like and trust."

Are You A Social Butterfly?

How do you act when you go to a networking event? Are you participating or merely a wallflower? How are you greeting and meeting people? If you don't join the conversation, no one will know who you are or what you do.

Let's look at a hypothetical scenario:

You are at a networking event hosted by an industry trade association or chamber of commerce.

You're dressed sharp, you feel good, and you're ready to enter the room, which is buzzing with all kinds of business professionals.

As you look around, you observe the crowd.

Oddly enough, there are a few people with bags over their heads; there's another group of people standing in the corner facing the wall. Then you notice a few people outside the building looking in through the windows. All these people seem to be on their own rather than engaging in conversation with anyone. These are what I would describe as "Lurkers" or "Spectators" on LinkedIn. They are the people who have a profile - may even scroll through their feed - but they don't make any meaningful outreach to others or create content on the platform.

Often these people are simply afraid of making the first move. It all starts with just one conversation. Just like in public with person-to-person contact, you find that one person you recognize or notice you have something in common. Finding someone you already know on LinkedIn and starting a conversation or commenting on someone's post is a great way to dip your toes in the water.

Next, you can't help but notice one character who is obviously "working the room," handing out business cards like a blackjack dealer, laughing a little bit too hard at their own bad jokes. The fast-talking card dealer is engaged in conversation, but you can't get a word in edgewise because they are talking more than listening. People are trying to avoid this person.

This person is putting quantity over quality. As a result, most of their business cards will end up in the trash. People do the same thing on LinkedIn with automated messages and sending as many connection requests as possible without any personalized note. And the result is the same - most of their messages will face the "delete" button.

The solution is the same in person and on LinkedIn - genuinely care. Take the time to ask questions, get to know people, and put them first.

You also might see the person going on and on about their divorce or their latest medical diagnosis. Oversharing is often confused with authenticity in the business space and can cost you credibility and business.

But then you notice a curious guest surrounded by a group of people actively engaged in a conversation. The curious guest in the center asks open-ended questions to get to know the others at the event.

So why are people naturally gravitating towards this person yet avoiding the others? It's because this person shows a genuine interest in others. This person listens far more than they speak.

Contributing to the conversation, being helpful, sharing your unique personality – that's what makes you memorable and outstanding. That's the type of person other people want to be around.

When it comes to LinkedIn, you can't just sit back and wait for people to come to you after setting up your profile. You're not going to get found without posting and sharing content, commenting, messaging, and other activities. Without being active, you won't show up in peoples' newsfeeds or notifications, either.

Give feedback, share insights, endorse a skill, compliment someone, check in with your network through direct messages, and be helpful to people. Be a giver, not a taker. Otherwise, you won't get invited to the next party.

> The Power of Giver's Gain[68] (a BNI philosophy) is all about focusing on how you can help people… and how that reaps dividends for you. To get more, you have to give more.

Above all, don't collect connections and then forget about them.

Building A Rapport

When forming new connections on LinkedIn, it's very much a cordial relationship – one-on-one person-to-person, human-to-human. People connect with people, not with companies. They can be loyal to companies, but it is the personal connection that binds people together.

> *"Sales solutions are easy once you identify the prospect's problems, concerns, and needs…with questions."*[69]

Continuing the networking event analogy, it's like meeting someone you instantly connect with at an event and then leaving the main group to sit at a side table for a deeper conversation. You discuss what you both may know and maybe even how you might help one another with an introduction or other beneficial gesture.

That's where a connection can be nurtured. The possibilities may develop towards new business opportunities either by referral or

---

[68] https://www.bnipodcast.com/2020/10/07/ episode-676-the-7-principles-of-givers-gain/

[69] Jeffery Gitomer, *The Sales Bible*

direct engagement. But you won't know this unless you start a conversation. Ask open-ended questions and listen more than you talk. That's why we have two ears and only one mouth!

The key to success is understanding the gap between problems you solve and why clients come to you and... clients' frustrations and what they want to improve. This is the secret sauce. Master this, and you will crush it!

> **Pro TIP:** Send a couple of personal messages each day to contacts you haven't talked with in a while to activate a conversation. Don't take it personally if they don't respond. They may not be active on the platform.

If you struggle with this, think about the person who makes you feel the most welcome and heard in your life. What kinds of questions do they ask? What tools do they use to make you feel at ease?

Are You In It For The Long Game?

Despite what you may have heard, LinkedIn is NOT a numbers game. Some people will disagree, but it is an opinion formed after watching some business owners succeed, and others fail. Although it takes longer to do what I suggest, the results will ultimately yield a greater return on your investment.

You may wonder if you've clearly identified the problem your prospects have that you have a solution for, how would they know about you if you don't pitch them?

The truth is that nobody wants to be sold to. Ever. So if they detect a sales pitch coming and they're not interested in what you have to say. Game over. Better yet, put yourself in their shoes. Would you want to be pitch-slapped? I think not. Yet it happens all the time on LinkedIn from people using automated scripted messages.

> **Pro TIP:** Ask intelligent questions that show an interest in really understanding prospects' and clients' problems deeply, and soon you will find they will start turning the tables on you and asking how they can hire you!

Social Listening And How To Use It To Your Advantage

One way to dip your toes in the [LinkedIn] pool is to pay attention to what your prospective clients are saying and their activity on LinkedIn.

This is called Social Listening.[70]

Start by searching for a few ideal prospects at companies you'd like to work with and observe their activity:

- What is important to them?
- What types of comments are they sharing?
- What are they reacting to?
- If their network is visible, look at who they are connected with?
- Who do you know in common?
- Is there something interesting on their profile to start a conversation?
- If they have recommendations, what do others think of them?

---

[70] https://blog.hubspot.com/service/social-listening

> **Pro TIP:** Create bookmarks of the activity pages for these profiles so you can easily access them.

Once you've done your homework, you'll see that it's not difficult to find things to relate with, and you may feel a bit more confident to test the waters.

The time is NOW to embrace LinkedIn. Don't let fear hold you back.

Use your voice to share interesting articles, respond to posts you enjoy, get your thoughts out there and see what happens. You can always edit or delete. And then build a better version next time. But you won't know until you try. It gets easier the more you do it.

Shortcuts To Growing A Quality Network

Hold on, haven't I been telling you there are no shortcuts to good relationship building? That is true when it comes to the relationship part. However, social media can still make things easier. And I am a big believer in "work smarter, not harder." So if you are ready to put in the time, these tactics will make it a little easier.

Opportunities On Linkedin

- **Identify Amplifiers** - find people in your target industry who are well connected and have a large audience that reaches your target audience.
- **Search for Relevant Content with High Engagement** - use hashtags, check profiles, and find posts that have activity amongst your target audience.

- **Join the Conversation** - share an insightful comment on these posts.
- **Experiment with Content Formats** - when sharing your own content, try a variety.
- **Conduct Polls** - an ideal way to find out about pain points. Polls are easy to engage with and take the pulse of your audience. Reach out to those who participate. Publish the poll results.
- **Pay Attention to Who Engages with Your Content** - click on the reactions and note who is commenting.
- **Look at Profile Views** - your activity will correlate to increased profile views. Check this often and decide the appropriate engagement.
- **Grow Your Database Based on Engagement** - when you see your target audience engaging with your content, this is your opportunity to build on that.
- **Connect with Everyone from Your Past Career Experiences** - colleagues, clients, educational institutions, trade associations, etc.

Cultivating Your Email Sources

- Export your contact list from your email client, select the ideal ones you want to connect with, and put them in an Excel or CSV file. Upload the file and LinkedIn will match the associated email with profiles and initiate a (generic) connection request without any message. Unless someone recognizes you, this is the equivalent of spam. WARNING: DO NOT sync your address book with your account.
- If you have a newsletter subscription list, upload the CSV file of those emails.

- If you have emails from the registrants of events you've hosted, upload that CSV list.

Doing Industry Research

- Look at the speakers for industry conferences, trade shows, and business events. Presenters usually have sizable audiences. Invite them to connect with a customized message mentioning the upcoming event. Once they connect with you, direct message them mentioning the event and your anticipated excitement hearing their talk. Stroking the ego goes a long way.
- Look at Top Executive lists in business journals such as 40 under 40, Rising Stars, Fastest Growing Companies, etc.
- Search for alumni from your college with specific job titles and connect with them.

Try them all! And then choose the methods of doing outreach that work the best for you. Every person has a little different communication style, and that will come across in your messaging.

How To Vet Inbound Connection Invites

It's tempting when being invited to connect, to accept all invitations. But you should proceed with caution.

As I mentioned in the first section, there are spammers and scammers on LinkedIn that you need to watch out for – and these are not only a waste of time but can be a security risk. Always look at the profile. If what you see makes sense and aligns with your strategy, then accept. If not, ignore. If it doesn't look right or appears to be a scammer, be sure you report it.[71]

---

[71] https://www.linkedin.com/help/linkedin/answer/1187

Take the time to look at the profile and ask yourself:

- Does their job title make sense with their experience and other information?
- Is their profile mostly filled out?
- Does their industry align with mine in any way?
- Do they have recommendations and endorsements?
- Are they connected to a reasonable number of people?
- If I don't know them personally, did they include a message with the invitation explaining why they want to connect?

And here's the thing, if somebody invites you to connect, it's perfectly acceptable for you to respond with your elevator pitch by saying: "Thanks for inviting me. Here's what I do. How can I help you?"

If they are just pitching, you'll probably not hear back from them. Move on.

The Difference Between "Connecting" And "Following"

Connecting with someone is a two-way relationship that requires one user to send an invitation and another user to accept. When you're connected to someone, you are both able to see each other's shares and updates on your LinkedIn homepages. You can also send direct messages to your connections on LinkedIn.

When you connect, by default, you also follow your connection. However, you do have the option to unfollow without removing the connection.

Following someone on LinkedIn allows you to see the person's posts and articles on your homepage without being connected to them. However, the person you're following won't see your posts. Likewise, when someone follows you, they have the same access.

You can reach a larger audience by allowing others to follow your activity and read what you're sharing on LinkedIn.

> **Pro TIP:** Once you reach 2,500 connections and receive more sales pitch invites than quality, change the default to FOLLOW.

Don't Miss Important Notifications

Make a habit of viewing your notifications daily. These are the first things I look at when I log on. You can personalize your notification settings,[72] and I highly recommend you take the time to make your notifications relevant.

Notifications are beneficial in two ways. For you, they are opportunities to engage with your network. Job changes, work anniversaries, and content engagement are just a few of the ones I like to respond to.

For your actions such as viewing a profile, endorsing a skill, or engaging on someone's post will in turn trigger notifications, thus providing visibility opportunities to those you want to be noticed by, assuming they check their notifications.

Review Your Newsfeed For Opportunities

Make a habit of viewing your newsfeed daily. Look at the posts that are getting high engagement (reactions and comments). Click

---

[72]   https://www.linkedin.com/help/linkedin/answer/76636/

on the reactions to see who is engaging. If you see something that catches your eye, there are a couple of options for actions to take:

- Add an insightful comment. Comments trigger a notification to all who previously engaged with the post.
- Look at the profiles of those who have commented on or reacted to the content. For profiles matching your target audience, send an invitation to connect with a personal message along the lines of:

"I noticed that you commented on [this post]. I thought it was interesting as well. Let's connect."

Always Customize Your Newsfeed

The content in your newsfeed is selected for you based on data-driven algorithms, the relevancy of your network, who you choose to follow, and targeted advertising of sponsored content.

The default is what LinkedIn determines as the most popular (top), or you can change it to show the most recent. It's also based on your connections and who you follow.

Improve your LinkedIn feed[73] by discovering new content and customizing your feed preferences. For example, by clicking on the three dots in the upper right corner, you can Mute, Unfollow or Turn Off certain notifications. In addition, you can follow companies and hashtags for topics you're interested in from desktop experience and the LinkedIn mobile app.

---

[73] https://www.linkedin.com/help/linkedin/answer/72151

Are You Ready To Get To The Top?

Everybody wants to connect with the C-Suite, especially the CEO. And the amazing thing about this platform is how many high-level people you can identify on LinkedIn.

According to LinkedIn Marketing Solutions, there are 61 million senior-level influencers and 65 million decision-makers on LinkedIn.[74] In fact, 4 out of 5 LinkedIn members drive business decisions[75] at their companies. So, no wonder everyone wants to connect with them.

Imagine from their perspective what it's like to be receiving all these requests to connect. That constant influx of requests is even more reason to give those senior-level influencers a compelling intention for your outreach.

But you can't always get to the decision-maker directly and make a connection. You have to surround yourself with people in their network first and become a 2nd-degree connection.

For example, my client is a Top 10 accounting firm that markets support services to smaller mid-market CPA firms. Ideally, they want to connect with the managing partner, but sometimes we can't get to them.

So what we'll do is connect with the other practice partners, the head of marketing, head of operations, head of HR, or other decision-making roles within the organization. It's fair to assume

---

74   https://business.linkedin.com/marketing-solutions/
      blog/linkedin-company-pages/2020/
      reaching-your-audience-on-linkedin-with-precision--a-primer--inf
75   https://www.omnicoreagency.com/linkedin-statistics/

that those people are connected to the practice leader. Once we have those connections, we establish a 2nd-degree relationship with our target audience.

At this point, once you've connected with decision-makers at an organization, you'll be better positioned to connect with that top person. They'll see you're already connected with their colleagues and are likely to accept your connection request.

> **Pro TIP:** Never consider someone "beneath" you - you never know what alliances and relationships are happening behind the scenes. That administrative assistant may be your ticket to reaching the CEO. Being kind and courteous to everyone is always a good strategy.

Action Items:

- [ ] Personalize invitations with WHY you'd like to connect
- [ ] Welcome new connections - start a conversation
- [ ] Harvest low hanging fruit with existing connections
- [ ] Don't collect and then forget your connections
- [ ] Check your notifications daily
- [ ] Master social listening to your advantage
- [ ] Use a surround strategy to get to your target
- [ ] Be cordial. Be helpful. Share your knowledge

PART THREE

ENGAGE

What does it mean to really **Engage**? Is it lead generation? Sales?

I would argue that it is learning to connect effectively with other people for mutual benefit - and the benefit on your end is to grow your business.

Yet, there's a new crop of people using LinkedIn like a cold-calling machine. They use automation, and pre-scripted blast invites using a "spray and pray" tactic. This past year it's reached annoyance levels so high that LinkedIn is flagging account activity and suspending accounts. Still, a few LinkedIn users use automated shortcuts to send out generic messages hoping a few will take the bait and respond. Their sole purpose is simply to pitch their product/services. It's a numbers game for them.

LinkedIn limits the number of outbound invitations that users can send out, as of publication invitations are capped at 100 per week. The number of invitations allocated to you is based on the number of invite acceptances you receive. You get a credit back for each invite accepted (similar to how it works with company pages and InMail credits).

Not only is the "pitch slap" invite annoying to the recipient, it's the quickest way to burn through all your potential opportunities.

Contrary to what some "experts" may try to sell you, using LinkedIn effectively isn't about flooding your sales funnel with leads and hoping a small fraction do business with you. This is the fastest way to damage your brand. And if enough LinkedIn members report you, your account will be suspended or terminated for good.

A more effective way to use LinkedIn is to define a strategy. Use a super-targeted approach to identify your ideal prospects - business owners and high-level executives... the decision-makers. Then build rapport so you can take the conversation offline eventually. Remember the three-legged stool!

Avoid Quick Fixes And Find Real Engagement

For everything you do on LinkedIn, there are humans just like you on the other end. The only difference is that LinkedIn is a global virtual network of business professionals. Use LinkedIn to find your audience. Build relationships and take the conversation offline, be it on a phone call, video conference, or an in-person meeting. LinkedIn is what you make of it.

If someone approaches you on LinkedIn claiming they can bring you "tons of leads," most likely they use methods that will get your account suspended. They focus on hacks, use automation and software tricks, spam members with "cold calling" outreach, and impersonal, generic messages – hoping that casting a wide net will bring in a few big fish. You might as well throw spaghetti on the wall and see what sticks.

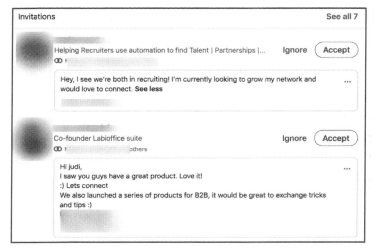

But you can't cultivate meaningful business relationships by spamming thousands of profiles. People know this trick, will recognize this, and will not respond. Aside from damaging your brand and bringing in just a fraction of qualified leads, those leads that do come from these types of mass outreach efforts are generally not good quality.

There's no shortcut to building credibility. One size does not fit all.

When you take the time to formulate your strategy, use a methodical, cultivated, and targeted – but natural – approach where you interact with your desired target audience. By being consistent and strategic, you will get results.

Your goal with everything you do on LinkedIn is to build credibility that leads to trust. Through your actions, share your expertise as it relates to your prospect's needs – enough so that they want to work with you or introduce you to people in their network. Use LinkedIn strategically to educate, inspire curiosity, and activate conversations.

> **Pro TIP:** Your primary goal when using LinkedIn should be to move the conversation offline to phone, in-person, video, etc. But first, you must build credibility to earn their trust that you're not going to pitch slap your sales offer.

Benefits Of Relationship Building

You can become a recognized expert in your industry – a thought leader – a subject matter expert – a voice in your niche – by proactively and strategically participating on LinkedIn. Moreover, you can still attain decent visibility organically (free) in LinkedIn's newsfeed.

When done the right way, starting with a strategic plan and a consistent effort, your visibility will increase, and prospects will begin to seek you out. All because they are aware of you as you've become visible. You established credibility through the content you share and are an authoritative resource who has a strong business network on LinkedIn.

The efforts you put forth will result in a predictable pipeline of referral business. You will have conversations with qualified prospects, speaking invitations, media interviews, strategic partnerships, and other opportunities to grow your brand, build your business, and get the recognition that will set you apart from your competition.

This section unlocks the secrets to **Engage** on LinkedIn more effectively, so you are ready to engage!

Working The Virtual Room

Do you know how to apply your real-life networking skills to the digital space? You will understand how the buyer's journey connects to your LinkedIn relationship and the step-by-step process to make this platform work FOR you instead of against you.

What NOT To Do (These May Surprise You)

These are the mistakes I see people making repeatedly - even those with experience. We will talk about the opportunities you may be missing, how to make sure what you are doing is strategic, and how to avoid becoming a spammer or scammer by accident.

Seal The Deal

ROI is important in anything that business owners do - and LinkedIn is no different. This chapter reviews how you should view (and neutralize) your competition, how to settle into the long game, and what to do when you are ready to close the deal with your ideal client.

Working The Virtual Room

I'll admit, you do have to get out of your comfort zone in order to be an active user on LinkedIn, and that can be challenging. I've witnessed my client's transformations, and with each action, they increase their confidence and participation. It takes work, but the rewards make it worthwhile.

I have a client that I've helped to generate nearly 100 leads. A lead is defined as a targeted individual who is responsive and interested in having a conversation. She's graded about a third of the leads as "A" quality - high probability and desired account.

The problem is my client isn't doing anything with them. She reaches out, and they show an interest in a conversation, but the call gets scheduled and then rescheduled, and the loop isn't closed.

After probing a bit, I found out her problem is that she's terrified to talk with these people who have expressed an interest because she doesn't want to come across as a salesperson. She doesn't know what to say without sounding awkward.

Here's how we tackled this obstacle:

- Together she and I review the "A" quality leads to prioritize them

- We identified 10 of the most promising prospects
- We viewed their profiles and activity to find common ground that would give us a starting point for conversation to make her more relatable

We listed out the objections her prospects might raise and role-played responses that worked through the various scenarios. Role-playing was to help her from jumping right into her solution but rather to empathize with and acknowledge the pain point from the prospect's point of view.

With this new information and added confidence, she's started commenting on their content, and it's generating positive activity. She circled back and messaged them to get a call on the calendar. Calls are now happening, proposals are being requested, and she closed her first deal as a result.

When you show a genuine interest in what matters to your prospects, they will notice and be receptive to your outreach in most cases. But it takes time. No instant fix here.

> **Pro TIP:** Be proactive about scheduling time for follow-up and outreach on your calendar or using your CRM.

Moving forward beyond the awkwardness and fear of failing requires breaking down a barrier to go from connecting with someone to trying to connect in a meaningful way. Sometimes that means breaking the overall task down into parts.

It's kind of like organizing your garage. You might not be able to do it all in one day. But you can start with clearing the workbench or unpacking five boxes from your last move.

It's the same thing with LinkedIn. Start with a small group of prospects and look for a common thread. If they respond to your message or show activity in their feed, you know they log on to LinkedIn and check their inbox. And, most importantly, they're receptive. Generally, people with premium accounts (gold LinkedIn icon) and recent activity will be a better batch to work with.

You want to spark *curiosity.*

That's a huge win — the percentage of people who respond after you send them a message is low — and you can't let that opportunity pass. It's a great sign when someone responds - it means they have a pulse (and check their inbox or notifications). But don't go for the kill at the first indication. Take it slow to build trust.

And don't take it personally if someone goes silent on you. There are a lot of possible reasons they didn't respond:

- They have other things going on in their life that have nothing to do with you
- They are not using LinkedIn actively or don't check their notifications
- They have changed their contact info and didn't update LinkedIn

If you've had previous interactions with them, you can give it a bit of time and try again. The main thing is you don't want to sound pushy or desperate. Put yourself in their shoes. How would you want to be approached? How would you respond? Mirror that behavior.

Why Are You Lurking?

According to Statista, there were 16.2% daily active users and 48.5% monthly active users in the United States as of March 2021.[76]

This means that many LinkedIn members are passive consumers, simply scrolling through the newsfeed and not much else.

Don't let this be you. Post content, comment, send messages, add new connections, etc. Let the world know who you are.

Engage with your connections from time to time. Sending direct messages creates relevance between you and your connection. Relevancy triggers the algorithm and helps your content show up in their newsfeed. Activate a conversation with your connection to stay top of mind. If you come across something that might be of interest to them, reach out to them. Or, if you're writing a blog post and want to get input, flatter them by asking their opinion.

When you post something, if someone takes the time to comment on your post – always respond to their comment – and try to use more than five words! These people are interested in you and your opinions and made an effort to post a comment. Comments increase the visibility of the post and push it back out into the newsfeed again. The more activity a post gets, the wider it expands in the feed. It's never too late to respond or comment.

---

[76] https://www.statista.com/statistics/194459/
frequency-with-which-registered-us-linkedin-users-update-profile/

Another way to grow your network strategically is connecting to the people commenting and reacting to your post. If they would make a good addition to your network, send them an invite message and mention your appreciation to them for taking the time to engage.

Breaking The 500+ Barrier

You've started gaining some ground on LinkedIn. You've connected with some quality prospects, and you're on your way to building a well-curated quality network. You've passed the first milestone of 500+ connections. Or perhaps you have a much more extensive network.

Regardless of the size of your network, the foundation of all this is to build trust. The following steps will help you move from virtual connections to real-world relationship engagement.

Step 1: Become visible by engaging with your network – so your best prospects know who you are.

Step 2: Showcase your expertise through quality content and insights you share.

Step 3: Strategically select specific connections for outreach based on probability and fit.

Step 4: Use content to establish your credibility and authority, ultimately leading to opportunity.

Let's break these steps down and look at this through the lens of real life.

Act As If...

When you first meet someone at a business event, there is idle chit-chat. Perhaps you're involved in the same groups, went to the same school, lived in the same geographic area, etc. You look to find that you share similar interests. And then there's looking for commonality to foster a deeper relationship. Find that common thread and ask open questions. Listen more than you talk. Pay attention to details.

If you engage with someone in a genuine way like this, you have a higher chance of expanding the conversation forward into a meaningful business connection. It's a two-way street. You give, and you get.

> **Pro TIP:** It's important to note that you won't try to make this transition with everyone. You don't have to pursue every prospect you encounter. In fact, you should be quite selective.

If you can help someone by making an introduction or a referral, that goes a long way. Pay it forward whenever possible. When you make a referral, broker an introduction, or give a recommendation, you lend that person goodwill.

The Buyer's Journey Is Not Linear

Often, I talk to clients who have been doing some of the things we covered and getting some great responses, but no new business yet.

You must remember - business-to-business marketing typically has a longer buying cycle than business-to-consumer. According to McKinsey's[77] study conducted at the end of 2020, the buying cycle has become even longer for B2B businesses since the

---

[77] https://www.mckinsey.com/business-functions/
marketing-and-sales/our-insights/
these-eight-charts-show-how-covid-19-has-changed-b2b-sales-forever#

pandemic. Longer buying cycles are because budgets are tighter and B2B buyers take more time to research **before** speaking to you.

89% of customer purchase journeys begin without seller input.[78]

Longer buying cycles are also why the content you share needs to support, not disrupt, the buyer research. 76% of buyers are now expecting more personalized attention from solution providers (YOU) based on their specific needs and problems.

The McKinsey study revealed that 70% of B2B decision-makers say they are open to making new, fully self-serve, or remote purchases in excess of $50,000, and 27% would spend more than $500,000.

Also, since 71% of buyers conduct a detailed ROI analysis before making a final decision, this needs to be considered part of your messaging.

In a B2B buyer's journey, there are typically multiple touches – it's accepted industry knowledge[79] that it takes an average of seven or more "touches" before a B2B buyer will agree to a meeting. Professional service contracts can be long commitments, so it's not a decision taken lightly. There may also be multiple decision-makers and/or parties who will influence the final decision.

---

[78] https://www.challengerinc.com/blog/
sellers-youre-not-getting-in-early-we-have-proof/
[79] https://www.oktopost.com/blog/understand-marketing-rule-of-7-b2b/

A methodical and deliberate approach to nurture and grow a relationship will drive desired results.

70% of B2B Buyers do their research online BEFORE talking with you![80]

When it comes to sales, B2B buyers typically move through six stages according to Gartner:[81]

Stage 1: **Problem identification.** "We need to do something."

Stage 2: **Solution exploration.** "What's out there to solve our problem?"

Stage 3: **Requirements building.** "What exactly do we need the purchase to do?"

Stage 4: **Supplier selection.** "Does this do what we want it to do?"

Stage 5: **Validation.** "We think we know the right answer, but we need to be sure."

Stage 6: **Consensus creation.** "We need to get everyone on board."

This infographic from Gartner does a great job of showing the interrelation of a B2B Buying Journey. It's not sequential, but rather simultaneous.

source: https://www.gartner.com/en/sales/insights/b2b-buying-journey

Winning In The B2B Buying Environment

So what does all this mean? It comes down to content. Your content. Gartner research found that buyers who perceived the information they received from service providers as helpful were three times more likely to buy a bigger deal with less regret. Let that sink in - three times more likely.

To win in this B2B buying environment, you should focus on providing buyers with content specifically designed to help them complete their buying jobs with ease. Inform, educate, and delight buyers with useful, actionable content. If buyers feel informed that they are making the best decision, then you've earned their trust.

Now that you know this and are aware of your buyer's pain points, you are informed and ready to start building relationships.

Your First Step

These are the steps I take when onboarding a new client:

Step 1: Optimize your profile to transform it from a resume to a resource for your ideal customer. Profile optimizing includes clarity on the pain points your buyers may be experiencing.

Step 2: Perform a content audit and create a content inventory library of your published work – articles, blogs posts, LinkedIn posts, videos, podcasts, etc. Creating a content library takes time now, but it also saves time in the long run.

By cataloging your content, you have a snapshot of the content you have to work with, what work needs updating and what holes need filling.

Since we've identified the pain points in optimizing your profile, we now need to understand how your content aligns with the problems your buyers are experiencing.

Step 3: Download your database of connections onto a spreadsheet, review them by company, and then target job titles.

As you review your database, it's helpful to add a column to mark who you know or recognize. Most people may only recognize or actually know only a small percentage of their connections. Reviewing your database is where having a "message trail" in your inbox helps you remember how you first became connected.

And it's interesting when you view them on a spreadsheet to see who has changed careers, jobs, retired, etc.

Step 4: From your list, identify your potential economic buyers and drill down to those who meet your ideal client criteria. Reviewing the connections you already have is considered the low-hanging fruit. Are they in a decision-making role? Are they part of a company you're trying to reach?

Now you're ready to formulate a strategy to reach out to them to activate the conversation. If you know each other, this should be easy. A simple message like: "*It's been a while. Would love to catch up.*" comes across more sincerely than a "scripted" outreach.

What about many of your connections that you do not recognize but who meet your target criteria? These connections may fall into the category you connected with but never did anything past making the connection. They have no idea who you are.

You'll need to formulate a messaging strategy to re-engage these people, and it must be unique to them. Look at their activity, read their profile and find a common thread. Then send them a direct message.

What you're trying to do here is activate a conversation.

If you just have connections you NEVER engage with, between you and me, what was the point of collecting and forgetting?

This approach is essentially a volley back and forth. Think of it as conversational tennis. Keep the ball in the air back and forth. You don't want to give them all you've got, in the first message.

Let it build up as you build credibility and trust in any business relationship. Gauge their interest. Never lead with your solution. You first have to understand where they are in need and pain point. Otherwise, they may ghost you.

Want an example?

When I meet someone for the first time, they often ask, "What do you do?" Rather than launching into a sales pitch, I respond, *"I could talk about myself all day. I'm interested in learning more about you and your business."*

This approach quickly shows them I have a genuine interest in them. You can take the same approach. At some point, the prospect will want to know about you. But now you understand where they are coming from and what their needs are. You can customize your message to be ideally suited to helping them understand how you could do business together - no sales pitch involved!

Beyond The Inbox - Taking The Next Step

The endgame of virtual networking on LinkedIn is to take the conversation into the real world – on the phone, in a video conference meeting, or ultimately in person, if possible. You need that conversational confidence to talk to your prospect eventually. And having a conversation is where credibility and trust begin. Don't blow it by going in too fast.

If your prospects ghost you on LinkedIn, it may be that they prefer other forms of communication. My Chamber of Commerce client finds that good old-fashioned phone calls or emails get far better results. Be creative and use other means like a personal email, a phone call, or even snail mail them a note. Your outreach needs to be received as a one-on-one engagement, not a spam blast coming from a marketing funnel campaign.

The fact is, only a small percentage of your connections will be responsive. It's much more valuable to have a few highly engaged prospects. This is why it is crucial to continually curate and expand your network selectively.

Action Items:

- [ ] Identify high quality leads on a regular basis
- [ ] Block off time to follow-up with those leads
- [ ] Avoid lurking or just taking up space - remember LinkedIn only works for you if you work it!
- [ ] Be engaged with your network on a regular basis
- [ ] Understand how the buyer's journey impacts your strategy
- [ ] Learn the art of conversational tennis
- [ ] Be ready to take the relationship beyond the inbox

What NOT To Do
(These May Surprise You!)

Most people think the biggest mistake you can make with LinkedIn is posting the wrong thing. Or commenting awkwardly. Maybe even connecting with a spammer. These happen but can all be easily corrected hiccups. You can always update a post, delete a comment, or remove a connection/unfollow someone who doesn't have a place in your strategically curated LinkedIn network.

I'm referring to the type of mistakes made at a basic level that can impact your entire LinkedIn strategy. But first, let's recap why you are on LinkedIn and what you hope to accomplish. Before anything else, define your goal of why you are on LinkedIn. Knowing your purpose on LinkedIn is the seat you sit on in the 3-legged stool of LinkedIn strategy. If you don't know why you are even on LinkedIn, you will struggle to customize the steps to growth.

Then you can put the Triple-E Method™ Strategy to work:

- **Elevate**: Build your profile and content to target your ideal audience
- **Expand**: Grow your business through effective networking

- **Engage**: Create meaningful conversations to close the deal

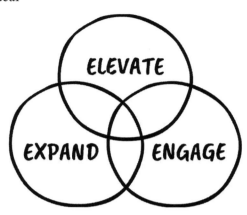

I see people trip up in each of these areas, so let's look at the most common ones and their fixes.

Mistake #1: Not Having A Strategy And Clear Purpose

By now, you've learned that LinkedIn is a powerful tool for networking, building relationships, and engaging with your audience. But without a strategy (aka a purpose), doing things ad hoc will quickly turn to frustration and you'll run out of steam. It happens. I see it all the time.

Success on LinkedIn is like balancing a three-legged stool. The three legs are your Profile, your Network, and your Engagement. All three legs are necessary to maintain balance. Without one of the legs, your efforts are hindered.

Your profile must align with your strategy. Otherwise, it is counterproductive for the creation of a quality network. If your profile is an incomplete hot mess, nobody will be able to figure out what you do and how you can help them. Remember, the attention span is mere seconds at best. Most times, they won't connect with you if you make them work too hard.

You must be deliberate and crystal clear when defining your target audience. If you think narrowing down your target audience will exclude your options, think again. Being specific will help you land better and more qualified opportunities. It makes it easier for your audience to see your relevance to their needs.

The bottom line is that your content must address the needs and the pain points of your audience. Your engagement with your audience needs to be relevant, informative, and insightful.

Mistake #2: Ignoring What You Already Have

LinkedIn is a rented platform, and your data, specifically your connections, are valuable to you. So get in the habit of downloading your records[82] regularly, at least monthly, or more frequently if you are actively adding new connections.

One of the first things I do with new clients is to look at their database of connections. Sorting this based on the connection's company name or job title, we can determine which ones align with the client's goals. Your connections are valuable resources, and they should go both ways. How can you be of help to them?

Once you review your existing network, formulate a plan to reach out to those people and engage them. It could be something as simple as endorsing a skill, so you pop up in their notifications. Or you could send a quick message like:

---

[82]   https://www.linkedin.com/help/linkedin/answer/50191

*"I thought I'd say hi. I was looking at your profile and
didn't realize you had left XYZ company and have moved
on. Hope you're doing well."*

Most people have a network with hidden gems. They just haven't
tapped into it yet.

Mistake #3: LinkedIn InMail Is Not The Way To Go

InMail messages are a premium feature that allows you to directly
message another LinkedIn member that you're not connected to.
Sounds like a backdoor to reach your prospects, right?

I am sure LinkedIn will not thank me for saying this and some
LinkedIn experts will disagree but receiving InMail's more like a
cold email. Nine out of ten times, the ones I have seen are blatant
sales pitches. The exception is when a recruiter uses them.

If you get one of these that you have no interest in, do not
respond - just ignore it and move on. If you do respond, it gives
the sender an InMail credit.

The only time it is worth it to pay for something like this (or
to cold pitch at all) is when you have exhausted all your other
options. How much sense does it make to get a ladder and put
yourself at risk of falling to reach the fruit at the top of the tree
when so many pieces of fruit are directly within reach? Go for
the proverbial low-hanging fruit by following up with current
connections, asking for referrals and introductions, and engaging
with great content. These steps will have far more benefit without
any of the downsides (or costs) of InMail.

Mistake #4: "Spamming" New Connections

When I first connect with someone, I usually respond with a short message to acknowledge the connection and to start a conversation. The worst thing you can do is jump right into your sales pitch. Your connection will likely ignore your outreach going forward. That's not a great way to start a relationship.

Some LinkedIn consultants use a scripted formula, similar to what one would do in a marketing multi-part drip sequence. This one-size-fits-all approach has been overused and abused one time too many times. It comes across as a sales pitch. Sure, it may save time and allow you to reach a larger audience (like a cold calling telemarketing hack), but it's a real turn-off to the recipient.

Don't do this.

Instead, take the time to customize your approach. Look at your prospects' profiles and base your outreach on some common thread within the individual's profile. What you have in common will be the cord that binds to help you build trust and credibility instead of damaging your reputation.

Once you've established some rapport, see where it goes.

Case in point - After a lengthy message volley with a new connection. I liked his style and I introduced him to two of my connections who would be ideal for him. He, in turn, made an introduction for me that turned into a paying client. Another recent example is a message dialog I had with someone where we established a rapport. It turns out his wife frequented my favorite pizza shop in Brooklyn. The next thing I knew, he invited me as a guest on his podcast.[83]

Take an interest in your network. Ask relevant questions to get to know them better. Build credibility and trust. Then, as you get to know them, you can reveal more and eventually move the engagement to a phone conversation, video call, or in-person meeting.

Yes, a customized approach is time-consuming. But if you aren't willing to put in the work, you probably should go back to cold calling! In the long run, the extra effort on LinkedIn will yield much better results.

It all goes back to establishing expertise, authoritativeness, and trustworthiness with potential clients. If you send generic spam messages – will you establish expertise... let alone become an authoritative and trustworthy source? No! But what you will do is damage your reputation.

Mistake #5: Not Leveraging Your Notifications

Review and optimize your settings and notifications[84] so you don't miss out on an opportunity to engage with your network.

If you don't have your notification set properly – say that pop up on your phone or in your email – set up correctly to let you know what new messages you've received, you won't get that message in a timely manner. As they say, the early bird gets the worm.

---

[83]   https://www.squareplanet.com/hays/

[84]   https://www.linkedin.com/psettings/communications

> **Pro TIP:** Send your notifications to whichever place (text or email) is likely to get your attention the soonest, so you can follow up quickly.

Your notification feed, depending on your settings, can alert you to milestones and updates with your network, such as work anniversaries, job changes, birthdays, who's viewed your profile, who's engaged with your content, who's posted recently, etc. Don't ignore these notifications.

A creative way to leverage milestone notifications is instead of using the default option (which most people do), "Congrats on the new job!", take the time to personalize your message to those you want to start a conversation with. Use that opportunity to ask them something related to their milestone. Don't simply send a generic message.

A colleague of mine created a word cloud using their profile picture to send birthday greetings. It's just another way to engage people and stay top of mind.

Mistake #6: Missing The Forest For The Trees

Often, we don't even realize when we are annoying. It is easy to let the pendulum swing too far from lurking to stalking if we are not self-aware and client aware.

The good news is that these are things we can practice and learn. And we get better the more we do it!

- **Be Crystal Clear on Your Audience Pain Points** - if it's relevant to them, you have their attention.
- **Make it About THEM, Not You!** - sorry, but your prospects care more about what's in it for them.

- **Lead to Your Solution, NOT With It** - if you take one thing away, this is it. Leading with your solution is selling, and that's a dead end.
- **Look at What They are Interested in and Engage** - take the time to find out what matters most to them and run with it.
- **Keep Messages Brief as if You are Texting Them Your Message** - if it looks like a canned script, you're most likely not going to get a response. Brevity is clarity.
- **Ask Permission - Never Send Links Without Asking** - think about how you feel when you get that blah blah blah spam in your inbox - that's a surefire way to damage a brand.

Mistake #7: Ignoring The Powerful Trio Of Three Dots...

Are you familiar with the three dots that show up when someone is typing? You know, they look like this ...

Most people NEVER click on the three dots. These three dots play an incredible role in the way you build your network, develop your brand and customize your content on LinkedIn. Every page on LinkedIn has these three simple dots to the right of a profile picture or in the top right corner of a post. This powerful trio of dots makes it easy to share a post, unfollow people who are no longer relevant, and more.

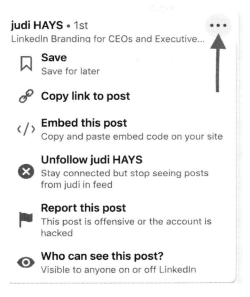

That is because they are full of additional actions to refine your experience.

When you text someone, and you see those three dots blinking back at you, usually you are in anticipation of what they are going to say next.

This anticipation is true when communicating online too. You always want to add value and then make them excited to see what is coming next. Think about how to keep that conversation going and get responses rather than talking until they are bored.

Mistake #8: Paying For Premium Features You Don't Use

People often ask me if it's worthwhile to pay for LinkedIn. The answer is "it depends."

There's a big difference between features, functionality, and filters between the free LinkedIn, the Premium level, and Sales Navigator.[80] If you are fortunate enough to be on a grandfathered Premium $29 plan from back in the day, keep it. But if you are paying more than that and you are simply lurking, then either take the platform more seriously or stop paying for what you're not using.

NO – LinkedIn Premium is a waste of money if you aren't growing your network. Likewise, if you don't care about profile views, don't actively share content, and don't use search functions for opportunities.

Every so often, if your account is eligible, you'll be offered a free 30-day trial of Premium. Take advantage of this upgrade directly to Sales Navigator because the features and tools are outstanding. After you've tried it for a month, you cancel Navigator. Note this in your calendar because they will charge your credit card on day 31.

YES –, there are good reasons to have a premium account, but like most recurring charges, we sometimes forget that we are paying for something that we might not be fully making use of.

Paying for your membership only makes sense if you have a strategy and a goal to use LinkedIn to grow your business and your brand. If this is the case, the Sales Navigator Pro (or higher if you have a sales team) is the subscription you would most likely benefit from. Pay monthly, not annually, so you can dial up and dial down based on your needs.

Pro TIP: If you cancel your Sales Navigator subscription, any messages, saved leads, searches and lists will be gone for good. This is why it's a best practice to keep all your communications within the basic LinkedIn platform.

Sales Navigator features that make it worth the investment:

- Notifications on updates to Saved Searches
- Advanced Search Capabilities
- Build Custom Lists of Leads & ABM
- Lead Recommendation
- Company Insights
- Exclusions for Refined Searching
- Job Changes
- Recent Activity
- Company News
- 90 Day Profile Views
- Unlimited Searches
- Real-time Sales Intelligence
- Smart Links for Sharing Content (Teams)
- CRM compatibility (Enterprise Teams)

Where Do You Need To Correct?

A quote from Winston Churchill states, "Success is not final, failure is not fatal, it is the courage to continue that counts." While he was dealing with much higher stakes than a LinkedIn profile, or even a business, the sentiment still holds.

Remember that whatever mistakes you make are almost always correctable.

The best way to avoid making mistakes is not to avoid taking any action - that just leads to nothing good happening either. The best protection you have is to be proactive in thinking through your goals, intention, and implementation. And, of course, try to avoid posting on social media when you are angry, sad, or tired. Make sure you have the mental space to approach each conversation with intention and thoughtfulness.

Action Items:

- ☐ Be clear on your purpose and use that to educate every part of your strategy
- ☐ Utilize the connections you already have before worrying about more
- ☐ Avoid LinkedIn InMail other than for very targeted reasons
- ☐ Don't spam new connections with an instant pitch
- ☐ Leverage your notifications
- ☐ Be self-aware and client aware to avoid becoming an unintentional spammer
- ☐ Make use of the Three Dots to personalize your experience
- ☐ Keep your clients engaged and curious with your communication

Seal The Deal

Likely you've gathered that the underlying point is that IT is about your client, not you. Now we finally get to the fun part – all about you!

The bottom line for being on LinkedIn at the end of the day is to grow your business. And that is okay! You provide unique solutions for your clients. You are able to help them in ways that only you can. And in order for you to grow and be sustainable to keep doing that work, you need to make money.

So what's stopping you?

In this chapter, we will talk about your competition (and why you don't need to worry about it) and how to close the deal once you have done the work to build the relationship.

Who's Your Competition?

I've heard numerous times that, "I don't have competition." I challenge that because we all have competition. Sometimes your competition can be inaction. Meister Eckhart said "The price of inaction is far greater than the cost of making a mistake."

Remember, when looking at your competitors, you need to consider both your direct and indirect competitors.

What do I mean by indirect competition? For example, if you are a company that operates trade shows, you might see other trade shows as your only competition. But in reality, maybe a client is not going to a different trade show - maybe they have decided to throw the towel in on trade shows altogether and do social media marketing instead.

Or, if you are Coca-Cola, you may only be watching Pepsi's decisions, but then you would be missing the large part of the market share that is not drinking soda at all anymore. Instead, your new indirect competitor is the sparkling water company.

Knowing the competition is where understanding your client's needs rather than simply their buying habits will help you grow and change your marketing or your business.

Make a list of the competitors you can think of. Then list your indirect competitors. And finally, in what ways are you competing with yourself in unhelpful ways?

Use this list to analyze your competitive advantages as we go through the rest of this chapter.

Why Does Your Competition Matter?

One thing you can safely bet on is that your competitors *are* on LinkedIn, thriving in your absence. They share insightful content, engage in conversations with your ideal audience, and land YOUR ideal clients.

Why let your competition take advantage of other opportunities while you watch from the sidelines? Indeed, a missed opportunity.

One thing is for sure – doing nothing is costing you an opportunity.

When it comes to LinkedIn, to reap the full benefits, you need to be actively playing in the game, not a spectator in the stands watching from afar.

When you are engaging intentionally and effectively, the competition becomes irrelevant.

The only way to know what makes you miss out on clients and business is to ask. First, ask yourself (from any deals you lost) what you could have done differently or better. Be honest.

And then, if possible, ask the company why they chose someone else. If a company considered you amongst a few other candidates, it never hurts to ask about the deciding factor. Sometimes that will make you grateful you didn't get the job. Or it may give you ideas of how to improve your response in the future.

It's scary to put yourself out there and ask for feedback but I have found that people are willing to share. You are framing the request from a position of wanting to learn so you can improve for the future. You see it all the time in those customer satisfaction surveys… what could we do better? Here's the thing, if you don't ask, you'll never know, and you'll keep repeating the problem.

> **Pro TIP:** If a client you have been nurturing gives their business to another company, ask who got the job and why. Asking the question can help build your referral network AND improve your approach going forward.

What To Do With Your Competition

You have a good idea who your competition is. What is unique about you compared to similar providers? Look at their websites, their profiles, search online to do your due diligence. Often this comes down to understanding the problem you are solving - going back to basics — and how your approach differs from the competition.

Competition is not bad if it helps us to learn and grow and be better. And sometimes it is not about better, but different. Are you making it clear what sets you apart? How do you solve the problems you solve? Do you lack trust or credibility?

There will always be things outside of your control, but knowing the factors involved in the first place helps you determine what is and is not in your control.

You may find your "competition" can become your biggest business asset.

In my work, there are lots of LinkedIn consultants. Most are great at what they do. In fact, I participate in several mastermind groups and group chats with other LinkedIn professionals. I view them as "Co-opetition," meaning that we cooperate and don't compete. There is so much of a need for our services and plenty of business to go around. This frame of mind allows me to refer business to others and vice versa. It comes from a mindset of abundance, not scarcity.

When you are clear about what makes you unique and what you have that no one else offers, this becomes easier.

Are You Present?

Post-pandemic, people are now more receptive to interacting with potential partners, clients, and professional service providers online.

And we know that LinkedIn is the ideal platform to foster and host cooperation and collaboration with decision-makers in B2B marketing. After all, 90 million LinkedIn users are senior-level influencers, and 63 million are in decision-making positions.[85]

What happens if you're on LinkedIn but not engaged - are you a spectator? Or do you have a lackluster profile that reads more like a resume and doesn't make the viewer curious enough to want to know more?

As a B2B company, if you're not maintaining an active presence on LinkedIn, you might as well not exist; you're invisible to your prospects. According to Statista, 49% of marketers use LinkedIn for marketing purposes in the US from 2017 to 2021.[86]

Suppose you have a LinkedIn profile, but it is not optimized with a "client-facing" presence that speaks directly to your ideal audience. As a result, you are missing out on opportunities akin to "leaving money on the table."

Maybe your LinkedIn presence is dormant or subpar. In either case, you're not on the radar. Your profile is like a house with overgrown weeds on a forgotten lawn. Without curb appeal,

---

[85]   https://business.linkedin.com/marketing-solutions/audience

[86]   https://www.statista.com/statistics/1094105/
us-marketers-using-linkedin-for-marketing/

you're not showing up in the feed. People won't just stumble upon your profile because you are there. You must participate actively.

Engagement Strategies To Activate

We have talked a lot about content, but this is the area that so many people miss.

Creating content always starts with choosing themes or subjects relevant to your target audience. A point to make here is that the type of content you create and share must be what your audience prefers. For instance, you may like to write, but your audience prefers visuals and videos. It's essential to understand the distinction between what you like and what your audience prefers. If it's not relevant to them, then you are simply talking to yourself. Audience preference is why measuring your content KPIs will help you.

Original content creation will set you apart from everybody else on LinkedIn. The fact is - most people don't publish anything. Or, at best, they may only comment or share third-party articles, so you automatically stand out when you go original.

Commenting on a post shows on your profile activity. It also appears on the newsfeed of those who engaged with that post. It may even send a notification to the originator of the post.

As you become more active and well-established as a consistent contributor on LinkedIn, you will naturally attract your target audience. Your audience will become curious and likely view your profile, perhaps reaching out to connect with you and ideally engaging with the content you share because they've seen one of your posts, videos, shared content, or comments.

Inbound leads like this are always more valuable – these people were looking for a professional service provider like you and your solutions. They sought you out, not the other way around.

Being active on LinkedIn in these ways is key to getting noticed and cultivating the right relationships. Simply by participating, you're training the algorithm, and you will be rewarded with visibility that leads to credibility.

When you find interesting content, don't just "like" it. That's a passive action. At the very least, use one of the reaction[87] options. Better yet, make an effort to add a comment as it relates to the post. Comments bring attention to the person who posted the content as well as everyone who has engaged with the post.

Make a habit to actively seek out content and regularly engage. This is where using the save and search function or hashtags can be useful in finding topical posts.

Prepare For The Long Game

Review your messaging and content to ensure it is most relevant and helpful to your customers and prospects.

Implement this on LinkedIn:

- Update your profile and Company page
- Fine-tune your "About" section
- Refresh your hero image banner
- Launch a brand awareness campaign

---

[87] https://www.linkedin.com/help/linkedin/answer/101466

Now be ready to do it all again. Some people resist the idea that they will have to keep working at their social media, specifically LinkedIn. But we don't eat one meal and assume we will survive until 100. We know we need to keep eating and replenishing. The same is true with our marketing. It needs to be fed a healthy and consistent diet of attention, or it will starve.

Know Thy Customers

Walk in the shoes of your prospects. And even go as far as knowing who your customer's customers are. Knowing your customers is where segmentation strategies can come in handy.

Implement this on LinkedIn:

- Use LinkedIn's advanced search filters for unique targeting to hone in on your audience
- Identify patterns, commonalities, and trends within the cohort
- Make use of LinkedIn's Account-based marketing tools in Sales Navigator

What key benefits does your competition bring to the table? How can you do better? Or how can you add something of value that your competition is missing?

Remember to keep in mind the intangibles. Some businesses particularly value working with small businesses, or family-owned, or minority certified/women-owned businesses.

Or maybe your processes are more environmentally sustainable. Perhaps you uniquely approach your process. Don't be afraid to use those intangibles as a selling point when they align with your client's values.

> **Pro TIP:** Make a list of all your tangible and intangible benefits to your clients and put it somewhere you can see it regularly.

Understand The Customer Journey

Now you know what motivates and interests your buyers. Take that knowledge to create content to engage with them at the various stages of their buying journey.

Implement this on LinkedIn:

- Regularly publish quality content on your Company page and personal profile
- Find content and respond to comments with insights
- Use polls to ask questions and then share the results with your point of view
- Take notice of the specific content your prospects engage with

Remember that sometimes a "no" just means "not right now." Being positive and keeping the door open can lead to long-term success.

Earn Trust Through Thought Leadership

Find ways to lean into your expertise to build brand awareness. Ask for feedback. Conduct research and surveys. Measure progress. Listen to the signals and identify the triggers. Take advantage of all your media channels.

Implement this on LinkedIn:

- Make use of LinkedIn Live
- Host a LinkedIn event (could be virtual or in-person)
- Share industry research on your newsfeed and Company page
- Recap trade shows, webinars, and industry events
- Compile industry-specific lists and resources – crowdsource user-generated content
- Feature your employee spotlights in videos and posts
- Find industry influencers to co-create content (podcast guests, etc.)

Ask The Right Questions

One of the most powerful questions in closing the deal is, "what do you see as the next steps?" Asking the right questions can help move the conversation forward without the pressure of a direct ask for the business. Such questions can also help you uncover any lingering objections or concerns they have so you can address them.

Taking the time to check in throughout the conversation can help make sure you are both on the same page and moving in the right direction.

This is just a sampling of the possibilities you can create to strategically engage with your prospects, your customers, and your team.

Using these engagement strategies will help you gain visibility as a thought leader amongst your audience and give you a clear point of distinction from any competitors.

Action Items:

- ☐ Determine who your competition is currently
- ☐ Figure out who your indirect competitors are
- ☐ Establish how you are better and/or different from your competitors
- ☐ Be present and active in engaging with your network
- ☐ Use content to establish your expertise
- ☐ Acknowledge that this is a long term rather than short term project
- ☐ Get to know your clients on a deeper level to continue to grow
- ☐ Learn to ask questions to move the conversation forward
- ☐ Become a great listener

Put Practice Into Action

Ione of these strategies will work unless you do! Now it is time to get started, and this final section will help you do just that.

How Often Should You Be Active On LinkedIn?

There are approximately 51% inactive users, according to Statista.[88] Don't quote me on this but I suspect at least 20% of the inactive users consist of duplicate or incorrectly set up accounts. The other 31% are people who may rarely sign in, if ever. And when they do, they just scan the feed and do nothing to engage. I've seen thousands of profiles, so this is just an educated guess.

All this inactivity means that there is an opportunity for you to stand out if you are among the active users. It's up to you, your availability, and your commitment to success to reach your goals.

Think of it as starting a workout routine. You start with small weights, and you build up strength through consistency and repetition. Your muscles get stronger, and you can do more in your routine. If you take on too much, you burn out quickly. However, if you lapse, you lose your mojo and have to start all over again.

---

[88] https://www.statista.com/statistics/194459/
frequency-with-which-registered-us-linkedin-users-update-profile/

> **Pro TIP:** If you do one thing daily, it should be to check your notifications and act accordingly.

What you do and the activity you put forth should align with your goals - expectations for why you are using LinkedIn and what you want to get out of it.

The main thing is to show up with consistency to "train" the algorithm. If your participation is random, then you will get random results. It's that simple.

Using the "in real life" analogy, your participation on LinkedIn is exactly like attending networking events and business meetings. Often you see the same people who show up time after time. You get to know them… maybe you'll work together, or you can refer business to them. But those folks who show up once or twice… nobody remembers their name. They haven't made an impression. They are simply bystanders.

For example, if you are looking to start conversations with your key prospects and build your network with quality connections that lead to business development opportunities, then you would do the following items daily:

- Check notifications daily and engage appropriately
- Respond to Inbox messages
- Acknowledge new connections with a message (don't connect and forget)
- Invite ten new people to connect with you to grow your network and increase visibility
- Re-engage with at least two existing connections daily (direct message, commenting, skill endorse, etc.)

- Share content in the news feed at least twice a week
- Find and comment on three interesting posts (of your target audience)
- Visit the profiles of your prospects before you reach out to them
- Keep your recommendations current – request one per month
- Endorse skills of your connections (for obvious skills)

All these strategies will help you connect with the right people and build a strong network with integrity that helps in your business development. If you have a "junky" network, you're going to have a more challenging time getting in front of the right people. But you can fix that by growing your network strategically.

No matter how you connect with people, always acknowledge new connections… a virtual handshake to make that first contact. Send them a message. Welcome them to your network. Thank them for accepting your invitation. You can do this at any time. You may be pleasantly surprised at the conversations it could lead to. It also gives you a message trail so you can remember how you first became connected.

Pro TIP: LinkedIn and Sales Navigator are two different platforms with separate inboxes and newsfeeds. Keep all of your outbound communications together on the regular version of LinkedIn. If you are on the paid subscription to Sales Navigator platform, take the time to open the profiles of anyone you find in your search using the "regular" LinkedIn platform. From here, you can choose the connect button to send your invitations and messages. Otherwise, you have to keep track of two inboxes, which can be time-consuming. And you might miss opportunities.

Social Selling Success

First, let's define Social Selling. According to LinkedIn,[89]

> *"Social selling is about leveraging your social network to find the right prospects, build trusted relationships, and ultimately, achieve your sales goals.*
>
> *The social selling sales technique enables better sales, lead generation, and sales prospecting processes and eliminates the need for cold calling.*
>
> *Building and maintaining relationships is easier within the network that you and your customers trust.*
>
> *To be successful in social selling, you must teach your prospects that the pain of the same is greater than the pain of change.*
>
> *To get your prospects to think differently about your solution is first to get them to think differently about their business.*
>
> *If you can do this in a way that leads to needs only your solution can provide, you will build trust and credibility."*

LinkedIn offers a ranking system using the Four Pillars of Social Selling. The Social Selling Index (SSI) is scored on a scale of 0 – 100 based on your LinkedIn activities relating to the four pillars of social selling. It is effective if you have a team of salespeople and want them to be competitive with the highest score.

---

[89] https://business.linkedin.com/sales-solutions/social-selling/what–is–social–selling

When you look at your SSI score, strive to be in the top 1% of your industry and network. Don't get caught up in putting a lot of weight on this score if it is above 75 because it's more of a tool for LinkedIn to give users something to measure.

How Do You Measure Success?

The best way to measure performance on LinkedIn is to tie your actions to metrics. Without specific metrics guiding you, there is no standard for measuring how your effort impacts your outcome.

How do you know what to measure? Start by answering these questions:

- What is your company-wide, time-bound business goal for the coming year?
- What is your revenue target for the coming year?
- What is your average deal size?
- How long does it take for a typical deal to close?
- How many new clients can you handle for the coming year?
- What is your conversion rate?
- What is your client retention rate?
- What is your proposal to close ratio?
- How many conversations do you need to have to reach your goal?
- What actions are you currently tracking – and not tracking – that are important to your business?

When evaluating content on your website, look for three things within your Google Analytics:

- What is the traffic coming to your website?
- What are they doing while they are there?
- Are they taking the actions you want them to (converting)?

Core Metrics

- Profile views – who's looking at your profile?
- How many invitations are you sending out weekly?
- How many invitations are accepted, and at what conversion rate?
- Do you have a plan to stay consistent with outreach to new people?

LinkedIn limits your outbound invites to cap at 100 per week. Typically, about 30% of your invites will be accepted. Factors impacting your conversion rate are the industry, your target audience, network size, profile, activity, and messaging.

If you are doing better than that – congratulations! But remember that quality rather than quantity is the key factor.

Get Familiar With Your Dashboard

If somebody interesting viewed your profile – check them out. If their profile matches up – invite them to connect with a personalized message.

Your weekly search stats will tell you how many times you appeared in results, where these searchers work, and what their job title is. Check this number bi-weekly to help you analyze both your short-term and long-term visibility. Are you being found by the right people? If not, consider revising your headline.

Keep in mind that if you set your settings to anonymous, you will not see who's viewing your profile.

Your Profile Views

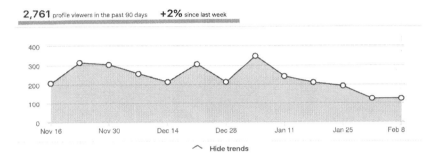

2,761 profile viewers in the past 90 days   **+2%** since last week

> **Pro TIP:** A premium account allows you to look back up to 90-days at people who viewed your profile. Compare that to a free account where you can only view the last five people who viewed your profile.

Your Dashboard, visible from your profile page, shows key metrics, including who viewed your profile and how many searches your profile appeared in. Go through this section regularly and track the results.

Your Dashboard
Private to you   ☆ All Star

2,761	1,703	232
Who viewed your profile	Post views	Search appearances

Metric	Definition	What does it tell you?
Who Viewed Your Profile	Clicking this number reveals specifically who has viewed your profile as well as an overview of where your viewers are from - on a premium account you can see views over the past 90-day period.	Profile views are good because it shows people are looking at your profile. This could be because you've invited them to connect, or because someone saw your article or post and wanted to know more about you.
Post Views	This shows the amount of views (reach) your most recent post has received in the newsfeed.	When your 1st level engages with your content, it shows up on the newsfeed of their connections (2nd, 3rd level).
Search Appearances	This shows your weekly search stats - how many times your profile has come up in a search	There are three important things to note here: Where your searchers work What your searchers do Which Keywords searchers used

Content Success

To determine if your content strategy is working, take a look at who is engaging with it.

At the risk of sounding like a broken record - it's not about quantity, but rather quality. It must be the right audience - your target audience. Try different formats. For instance, instead of posting a link to a blog post you've written, try just sharing a few lines of text that get to the gist of the concept. Just text - no link.

Track your content engagement so you can see what themes, formats, and criteria work well. If you have a popular post that is "evergreen," repost it. If it performed well before, chances are it will continue to perform well. Keep in mind, only a small percentage of your followers (about 10%) see your posts in their newsfeed. The views expand based on who engages with your content.

Let me give you an example. If people comment, react, or share an article I write, I make sure to reach out to them directly.

If we are already connected, I can send them a note and thank them.

But if we are not already connected, this is a great opportunity. First, I will check their profile and make sure they align with my overall LinkedIn strategy. If they do, I can send a connection invitation with a personalized message.

In this case, it is important that I let them know how I found them (the comment, share, etc.) to establish credibility.

If they accept my invite, I'll reply with a welcoming message, just as you would if you met someone in person. Over time, if it makes sense, I'll engage with my new connection and their content to see how we can further the relationship.

Don't be creepy – but do engage as a human being, not an automated bot. And always respond to anyone who takes the time to comment.

Get Them To The Next Level

LinkedIn is a handy platform to create a name for yourself. It's the most robust virtual networking site and a top spot for building B2B relationships. But it's not the end-all, be-all platform.

You don't own LinkedIn like you do your website or your email list. LinkedIn is essentially a rented platform, and the rules can change - and they do – and you have no control like you do on platforms you own. So at some point, you need to take the conversation off LinkedIn, but you need to do it strategically.

Your next step should be to drive your traffic from LinkedIn to your website with valuable content. Don't have a website? Why not? They're very easy to create.

> **Pro TIP:** Consider having a place for visitors to sign up to join your email list. Offer them something of value in exchange.

One last takeaway:

The #1 mistake is not being yourself. Building quality relationships on LinkedIn is all about authenticity. Without authenticity, you can't build a reputation for expertise, authoritativeness, and trustworthiness.

Remember, LinkedIn is NOT a selling platform. It's a relationship-building network.

If you strictly want to sell and generate leads without any engagement or effort, then LinkedIn Marketing Solutions[90] (paid ads) is a better strategy for reaching your goals faster.

Growing and nurturing relationships takes time. But it's time well spent because, like a great marinara sauce, slow and steady, it yields the best long-term result.

Action Items:

- [ ] Check your notifications daily
- [ ] Always acknowledge your new connections
- [ ] Keep your messaging within the free version of LinkedIn
- [ ] Benchmark your Social Selling Index and check quarterly
- [ ] Check "who's viewed your profile"
- [ ] Consistently grow your network
- [ ] Get familiar with your dashboard
- [ ] Track your content engagement

---

[90]   https://business.linkedin.com/marketing-solutions

Conclusion

Linkedln is where business professionals go to find other business professionals. It is the premier social platform for connecting virtually with a highly qualified B2B network. You engage, connect, and build profitable relationships with your best prospects. This is where the right type of prospects will look for you. It's the ultimate virtual networking event.

My hope is that the content in this book has demonstrated that LinkedIn is a tremendously powerful resource for building your business – a fundamental component of your marketing and business development strategy. But the key here is that you must start with a strategy and commit to being consistent.

When you engage consistently, you can expect a steady stream of people you can follow up with – turning those people into referrals and business opportunities.

If you're not on LinkedIn – or if you are but not active in the right way – you're invisible to those B2B buyers you're trying to connect with. You're missing opportunities and leaving money on the table. I guarantee your competitors are filling the void.

It's easier to do than you think… Try it and see for yourself. Start with the process of setting up a strong profile and connecting with potential clients.

Best Practices For Growing Your Business

- Commit to a Routine
- Determine Your Prospect Persona
- Position With a Client-Facing Profile
- Develop a Content Strategy
- Develop Your Leadership Platform - Be a Giver
- Spend Time Engaging With Decision Makers
- Use LinkedIn Search and Boolean Strings to Find Your Prospects
- Grow Your Network Strategically
- Systemize & Simplify Activities
- Set Your KPIs and Measure Your Performance

Use LinkedIn to identify your target audience and engage with them, but have your end game be to move the conversation off of LinkedIn.

Cultivate and grow your platform so you are not beholden strictly to the whims of LinkedIn's terms of service. LinkedIn can and does update it's algorithm and settings regularly, so don't get caught unprepared.

Be aware that LinkedIn frowns upon using any automation tools, whether AI cloud-based or browser plug-ins. These may be "time savers," but they are a sure-fire way to get your account suspended, and you could lose the progress you've been making.

Quick Recap - Your Key Steps:

Step 1:   Determine your ideal customer

Step 2:   Identify their pain points

Step 3:   Position your brand with a client-facing profile

Step 4:   Develop a content strategy to align

Step 5:   Build your leadership platform

Step 6:   Find prospects who fit your target criteria

Step 7:   Grow your database strategically

Step 8:   Set up your messaging script prompts

Step 9:   Develop a system to manage all these activities

Step 10: Join the conversation and engage

Step 11: Nurture your leads throughout the sales cycle

Step 12: Activate your existing network

Step 13: Follow up, follow up, follow up

Step 14: Track your KPI and adjust accordingly

Thank you for reading along and letting me be a part of your business journey! I look forward to hearing how you put the Triple-E Method™ to work for you!

Resources

Linkedin is an ever-changing platform – like most social media these days.

It is necessary to stay up to date. That is why I created a webpage just for that purpose – so you can get all the latest and greatest that LinkedIn has to offer!

When you go to JudiHays.com/bookupdate and enter your email address, you will be able to get free resources for LinkedIn as well as updates for this book and news of new features on LinkedIn.

Be sure to connect with me on LinkedIn at www.linkedin.com/in/judihays and mention this book.

LinkedIn Customer Support

This might sound counterintuitive, but it's the best way to get a quick response. When you have a quick technical question, LinkedIn's Twitter account is specifically for customer support requests – access it on Twitter @LinkedInHelp.

Additional LinkedIn Resources

https://linkedin.com/help/linkedin
https://business.linkedin.com/sales-solutions
https://business.linkedin.com/sales-solutions/blog
https://engineering.linkedin.com/
https://business.linkedin.com/marketing-solutions

Acknowledgments

I almost didn't write acknowledgments because I know I will forget someone. But I also know this book would never have happened without the help of so many people.

First, a big thanks to my clients. They have taught me as much as I have taught them and given me a space to prove that these strategies and ideas work. You push me to be better and improve every day. I'd also like to thank my co-opetition, all the LinkedIn trainers and strategists who openly share their insights and discoveries for the greater good. Special thanks to Brynne Tillman, who I credit to teaching me the fundamentals of social selling, Phyllis Khare who provided me the training to fully understand the power of social media through Social Media Manager School. Also in no specific order, I have learned so much from LinkedIn experts Isaac Anderson, Monte Clark, Jeff Young, John Esperian, Angus Grady, Mike O'Neil, Susan Tatum, Mandy McEwen, Joe Apfelbaum, Brenda Meller, Jared Wiese, Jo Sanders, Nigel Cliff, Sandra Clark, Sid Clark, and AJ Wilcox. This book never would have made it to print without the help of my team including Rivka Hodgkinson who helped organize, edit, revise, and refine the contents of this book and to Steve Gordon and his team at Unstoppable CEO Press for getting this DONE!

About the Author

J udi Radice Hays is an authority on marketing strategy and a certified LinkedIn strategist. She has invested the last 30 years in the study and application of selling high-ticket services. Judi helps business leaders and companies build authority, credibility, and trust, ultimately increasing revenue. Judi sells Results!

Judi teaches her proprietary methods through workshops, team training, trade industry associations, seminars, consulting, and white-glove 'done-for-you' services.

She is a Forbes contributor and a Forbes Business Council member. Judi consults with businesses in 30 different industries, all selling high-ticket products and services in high-trust selling environments. Judi consults, strategizes and does things for her clients they can't do for themselves.

Judi is also a frequent podcast guest and speaker. She has presented trainings and seminars for FENG (Financial Executive Network Group), CORENET (Commercial Real Estate Network), Greater Austin Chamber of Commerce, NWBC (National Women's Business Council), NAWBO (National Association of Women Business Owners), SBA (Small Business Administration),

SCORE (Service Corps of Retired Executives), NAPO (National Association of Professional Organizers), and Baruch College.

Keep Learning

Blog: https://judihays.com/category/blog/
Download the FREE companion worksheets for THIS book at: https://JudiHays.com/bookupdate
Read Judi's Forbes articles[91]

Connect With Judi On Social

LinkedIn: www.linkedin.com/in/judihays
Twitter: https://twitter.com/askjudihays

Book Me For Speaking And Training

Judi Radice Hays is available for speaking and training engagements. To have Judi speak to your group, either at your event or via webinar, or to provide training for your team, go to email judi@judihays.com.

Spread The News!

Since you've made it all the way to the end of this book, I hope you've learned a new approach to elevating your personal brand on LinkedIn. If this book has brought you some value, I would appreciate your support in letting others know. After all social proof is the best kind!

Profile Hot Seat

If you have goosebumps while reading this book, or feel inspired to put these insights into action, then get into the Hot Seat.

---

[91] https://www.forbes.com/sites/forbesbusinesscouncil/people/judihays

Want to find out how your personal brand is aligned with your audience? Apply for a Profile Hot Seat with Judi Hays and find out.

To schedule your Profile Hot Seat, go to: www.judihays.com/apply

Testimonials

As usual, I don't expect you to take my word for it! Here's what my clients have shared:

> *We have been working with Judi for over a year now and have made significant progress in our LinkedIn B2B campaign. She understands how the LinkedIn algorithms work and when they change -- then applies that learning to our LinkedIn efforts. She and her team have become our "back office" to keep our content fresh and has encouraged me to step out and provide new forms of content I probably wouldn't have done on my own.*

Kevin Poppen, CPA, RSM US LLP,
Senior Director

> *Judi is innovative, clever and is always looking for ways to improve the client experience and outcomes. Her thirst for knowledge is inspiring, and her gift of knowledge is priceless. Judi's tireless commitment to getting results is what makes her clients so successful. I am looking forward to working with Judi for years to come.*

Brynne Tillman, Social Sales Link, CEO

Judi has been a huge part of our team for nearly 2 years, and has been quite instrumental in our desire for measured organic growth. She brings an ideal mix of marketing strategy, pragmatic approaches and tactics, personality and organization to our boutique consulting firm. Judi also is brilliant on ways to nurture client relationships on the LinkedIn platform without 'selling' to anyone.

Brad Forester, JBF Consulting, CEO

"I have only been working with Judi for the past 5 months but have learned so much about LinkedIn and more than DOUBLED my network! Judi has provided great content, marketing strategy and coaching. Her ability to find new ways to reach people is unmatched. I love working with Judi and highly recommend her to anyone struggling to find new opportunities or is new to networking on LinkedIn."

Richard Bova, CEO and Technical Director, NetOne

"Judi is an absolute rock star! She applies her deep marketing expertise to provide specific actionable recommendations to optimize your LinkedIn profile. I spent some time with her for a diagnostic review, and I learned a lot in a short period of time. She brings very positive energy and a contagious can-do attitude to her work. I highly recommend Judi to anyone who wants to get more out of LinkedIn."

Lawrence Van, CFA, CVS Health

"Bringing strategic thinking and boundless optimism, Judi Hays is truly a force to be reckoned with! She offered invaluable expertise on LinkedIn marketing issues, expert guidance on profile optimization, and savvy ideas on engagement that transformed how I use the LinkedIn platform. I highly recommend her to anyone wanting to maximize the possibilities of LinkedIn."

Mari Fukuyama, Senior Vice President, Barolet Associates

"I wanted to thank you for the awesome course yesterday and thought it only appropriate to do it through LinkedIn. I love how you are strategic and tactical at the same time -- very few people are." If you're looking for a LinkedIn expert, I could not recommend Judi highly enough.

Gavin McMahon, Chief Learning & Product Officer, Founding Partner, fassforward

"Judi is one of the most knowledgeable people on the planet when it comes to LinkedIn. I highly recommend that you follow or connect with Judi. She WILL teach you something you need to know about LinkedIn."

Jeff Young, #TheLinkedInGuru, Professional Networker, LinkedIn Trainer

"I've worked with Judi on multiple marketing projects. Her knowledge of LinkedIn is second to none and her energy and enthusiasm is infectious. What I appreciated most about her, however, is how she captures the voice of what's needed on social media. So much spammy, sales-y messages get posted on this platform, destroying any sense of

interpersonal connection. Judi doesn't do that but retains a true conversational tone with professional integrity. And she's a joy to work with! I heartily recommend her expertise."

Bill Zipp, Bill Zipp Leadership Link, President

"Working with Judi was an amazing experience! She's an expert in her field, full of knowledge and she extended herself above and beyond. Judi is very insightful and completely transformed my LinkedIn profile to attract the correct audience as well as providing strategies on how to make the best use of the platform. She made the whole process simple and straight-forward, so it was easy to understand yet her method and approach is highly effective! I would definitely give Judi the highest recommendation possible and would advise anyone to work with her as she's truly a pleasure. I look forward to continuing the partnership!"

Victor Egbuna, Bodyworks for Your Health, CEO

"OMG! I worked with Judi for 2 hours and embraced the concept of meet, greet and feed. Together we tackled the process of identifying prospects, messaging and connecting. GAME CHANGER!"

Ed Burzminski, Chamber Marketing Partners, Inc. Strategy, Growth and Operations

"Judi is ONE OF A KIND. If you are looking for a motivated MARKETING expert that REALLY takes the time to SERVE the people in her life, look no further. Judi is a total rockstar. She is engaging, fun, smart, easy going, honest, hardworking, committed, loyal and very responsive. You know from the second you have a conversation with her that SHE GETS THINGS DONE. If you have a marketing project, need support, want to grow your business, JUDI can help you. Setup a time to talk to her and you will be inspired. Thank you, JUDI, for all that you do :) BOOM"

Joe Apfelbaum, Ajax Union, CEO & Founder of B2B Digital Marketing Agency

"Judi is a LinkedIn Networking Dynamo! Judi joined us at Baruch College as a guest speaker in the Digital Marketing class for masters students last Friday and completely blew us away with her insight, energy and tips. You think you know about LinkedIn until Judi shows you the way! I am excited to fine tune my profile further with Judi's rockstar recommendations on personal branding, searchability and making meaningful connections online."

Dana Humphrey, Dana Humphrey Life Coaching, Life Coach

"My company has been working with Judi for 2 years. Starting from virtually nothing, she has helped us develop, execute and refine a LinkedIn marketing strategy that resonates with our target audience while enabling us to carefully build and cultivate our brand. Judi has an intuitive understanding of what works and what doesn't, which enables us to achieve

results without wasting effort. In short, we are highly reliant on Judi for her digital marketing expertise, and I would recommend her without hesitation."

Mike Mulqueen JBF Consulting Partner, JBF Consulting Strategy Practice Lead

WOW! Judi's a wiz when it comes to LinkedIn strategy! In our working session, she rattled off a ton of top-level things for me to do immediately and then some deeper dive solutions to enhance both my personal profile and my business page. She's the bomb—big heart, super smart and very generous with her time. Don't miss a chance to get some of her wisdom—you won't regret it!

Andrew Mellen, Declutter and Organize Your Life, Andrew Mellen, Inc. Keynote & Motivational Speaker

"An hour and a half with Judi was like a weeklong boot camp with a lot of other "experts". She has a way of making things easy to understand and delivers actionable tips to help you solve any problems that she helps identify. Business aside, I really enjoy my interactions with Judi. She's authentic, knowledgeable, kind, and endlessly helpful. Thank you so much for being you!"

Austin Grammon, SpeakerFlow, President

"One conversation with Judi was all it took to know that she is just the type of person I want to work with: She's honest, knows her subject matter, generous with her time, and actually cares about my success. I recommend her without reservation."

Tom Rubens, Inclusive Idaho, Board of Directors

"I had my first call with Judi today and I am certainly glad I did. She is an information powerhouse and gave me a ton of useful information. I appreciated her cheerful demeanor and how she applies her listening skills to immediately grasp the subject matter. Judi is a gem!"

Karen Avery Marchetti – LION Avery Grace Careers, Career Coaching, Resumes and Outplacement

"Judi helped me improve my LinkedIn profile in dozens of ways. Within a few weeks of making her recommended changes, views of my profile, posts and articles more than doubled, with views of some posts increasing tenfold over the average to that point. Judi is professional, adept and very conscientious with her clients; I highly recommend her services to anyone looking to boost their LinkedIn presence."

John Foster, Wolf + Associates, Organic Specialists Senior Associate

"Judi is awesome. Our weekly conversations are the highlights of my weeks. I view her as both a marketing consultant and a business coach. She helps me think though concepts and evaluate opportunities and approaches. She is particularly effective in helping me refine concepts and crystallize business cases. Her follow through and commitment are not just good but outstanding. She cares deeply about her clients and is focused singularly on delivering unique value."

Rob McIntosh, McIntosh Search, President

Index